Total Gonzo Poems

Total Gonzo Poems

By Charles Giuliano

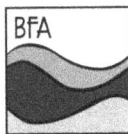

Berkshire Fine Arts, LLC
Adams, Massachusetts

BFA

berkshirefinearts.com

For Astrid Hiemer, my partner and muse, who has been with me through every step of creating this collection of poems. And gratitude for my Irish and Italian ancestors and extended family. They came to America for a better life and aspects of first *Shards of a Life* and now *Total Gonzo Poems* document and celebrate their colorful history and accomplishments.

Contents

Introduction xi
First Use of "Gonzo" July 3, 1970 xvi
Acknowledgments..xix
Gonzo Shine..xxi

Family 1

Crosscurrents 18
Ancestors 20
Patrick Nugent... 22
Good Harbor Beach... 24
Beaver Dam Farm... 26
1913 28
James Flynn 30
Family Business...32
Irish Lads 36
Baylor Bullies..38
On the Porch 40
Visit...42
Letter 1940 43
Sweet Dreams 46
Garden of Eden 48
Trim..50
Son et Lumière...52
Bouillabaisse 54
Cancer 56
Pippy...58
Let Her Eat Cake 60

Lotus...62
Pesto...64
Irish Spring 66
Bris 67
Samson...68
Uncles 70
Uncle Freddy 72
Freddy's Music Unlimited 74
Twilight of the Don 76
Father's Day..78
On the Road...80
Spotty 82

Astrid 84

Fireworks..85
Kerouac 88
Under the Apple Tree 90
Cake...92
Oceans 93
Trees...94

Friends 96

Amigos 97
The G 100
Alice's Breast Flaunt...102
Not Plain Jane 104
Touch of the Poet...106
Martin Mugar..108
Geoffrey...110
Smoki Bacon...112
Consigliere 114
Tampa 116

Music 118

Diana Ross 119
Sexual Healing..120
Tommy..122
Miles...124
Ornette...126
Philip Glass 128
BB King...130
John Cage..132
Bethel 134
American Pie 136
Tulips 138

Basement Tapes **140**

Coptic Pot..141
Agitprop...142
Dust Bowl...144
Hearts 146
Shards 148
WILD..150
Shango 152
Diocletian 154
Ankhhaf...156

Omnibus **158**

Every Other Sunday 159
Hook 162
Son of a Beach...164
Old Mr. Boston 165
Hippy 166
Duck 167
Y Not...168
Movietone News 170
Reasonable 172
Guido's..174
Lobster Thermidor...176
God Is Dead 178
Lights Out 180
Kiss Me Kate 182
Bang Bang 183
Apathy 184
Fear Eats Itself 185
Making Art 186
Beauty of the Beast 188
Sisyphus Now 190
Big Easy 192
Tennessee Williams' Hotel Plays 194
Ms. Divine...196
Killing Time...197
On the Beach..198
Bistro...200
Luck of the Non-Irish 202
To Ur is Inhuman..203
Jihad..204
Adams...206
Noblesse 208
Jingle Bells 210
Tats..211
Daily Scam 212

Faux 213
Rejuvena 214
Woody 215
Valentine's Day 216
Rubenesque 217
Beckett Busted 218
Charity 219
The Mount 220

Gonzo 222

Out of the Blue 223
Nudie 225
First Novel 228
Wild Party 230
Max's 232
Mad Max..234
Pop 236
Summer of Love 238
Reverie 239
Fence 240
Murder Building 242
Birth of Gonzo 244
Easter 246
Bob Fowler 248
Harry Bikes 249
Chris Burden..252
Up the River 254
All Dolled Up 256

Seasons 258

February 259
Noah Snowah...260
Nobirds 261
East Boston Blizzards...262
March 263
April..264
May 265
Monty's..268
June 270
July..271

Introduction

The challenge to write poetry and post it to *Berkshire Fine Arts* started in August 2014.

That resulted in the first book *Shards of a Life*, which was launched with a reception and reading on the porch of Edith Wharton's The Mount the following June. There the Mount's director, Susan Wissler, interviewed me and I read selections from the 100 published poems.

Precisely a year later, in August 2015, I completed this collection of 139 Total Gonzo Poems.

Gonzo is a word that I coined while telling an outrageous story to a gathering with friends of the now deceased Bill and Susan Cardoso. At the time Bill was the editor of the *Boston Globe Sunday Magazine*. There is a poem about that occasion in this book.

On July 3, 1970, I used the word gonzo for the *Boston Herald Traveler* in my review of the rock band Ten Years After at Harvard Stadium. It was the first published use of "gonzo," a word that has made its way into the American vernacular and is included in multiple dictionaries.

For example, the entry for *gonzo* in the eleventh edition of *Merriam-Webster's Collegiate Dictionary* is: gonzo \ gän-( )z \ adj. [origin unknown] (1971) 1 : idiosyncratically subjective but engagé <~journalism> 2 : BIZARRE 3 : freewheeling or unconventional esp. to the point of outrageousness <a~comedian>.

That review in its entirety is included in this book.

Much has happened in the 45 years since then.

Cardoso famously dubbed Hunter Thompson a gonzo journalist. In a letter he commented on Thompson's "The Kentucky Derby Is Decadent and Depraved," which was written for the June 1970 *Scanlan's Monthly*, as "pure gonzo journalism." When asked, Cardoso claimed gonzo as his invention, which is not accurate. There is no debate that he expanded and promoted it as Gonzo Journalism.

Both Bill and Hunter were true exponents of all things gonzo. Their writing was outrageous, crisp, and defied all the norms of mainstream reporting. Much of the inspiration was fueled by a massive intake of drugs and alcohol.

Because I earned my keep in academia, the pursuit of gonzo was more restrained. Twenty years ago I stopped taking a toke before writing a piece. I was surprised to discover that it did not change the work. I had found a better muse in my wife, Astrid. We constantly inspire each other and share our creativity.

While Hunter was widely known, Bill struggled to make ends meet. On many levels he was no less brilliant and inventive. What survives of his work is a collection of pieces published in the wonderful and insightful book, *The Maltese Sangweech*. It should be required reading for journalism classes.

This second book was motivated by an effort to reclaim a fair share of the gonzo legacy. The challenge was to develop the gonzo style into poetic form. My consigliere and daily communicant, Robert Henriquez, in the essays he has written for these books, has placed the work into a literary and creative context. I am deeply indebted to our dialogue, which has provided shape and form to these efforts.

As the poems emerged, Astrid has read them to me with spontaneous suggestions for edits. She has been the constant first responder, just as I have been for her work.

Leanne Jewett has served as a superb editor and consultant to these projects. She has provided the safety net of another pair of sharp eyes. Amanda Hill has been a fabulous designer of the books.

As the writing evolved, it has morphed into being more than just gonzo.

There has been a prolific frenzy of almost daily postings. The ready access to the work on our site, *Berkshire Fine Arts*, has made this a transparent and visible process, and sparked constant feedback from friends and other poets. This has resulted in shaping and focus. This is the reverse of the usual approach by which authors write books of poetry. Normally the work is not read until it is published and then by a small audience of readers.

Posting to the website has allowed for an ongoing critical dialogue. Depending upon the subject, there has been, at times, feedback within minutes of posting. So there is a constant sense of what does or does not work.

Recently, when I met with a friend for lunch, he asked how the book was coming. I said that it was about finished, but I wondered if there would be a third. Has the well gone dry? These first two books, a kind of segmented autobiography, have explored the low-hanging fruit of colorful anecdotes and life experiences.

The two books have delved deeply into ever-darker family history. There has been research about my Irish ancestors, The

Nugents of Rockport, which entailed finding images from decaying family albums—photographs that have faded and require Photoshop work to make them legible.

Many of the pictures contain photographs of relatives who are difficult to identify. It has been even more challenging to piece together the images and history of my Sicilian family. Those photographs were mostly taken by my mother during the early years of marriage in Brooklyn. After a few years she returned home to Boston. There I grew up with the Nugent/Flynn clan and only saw Brooklyn relatives when they came for holidays or vacationed in Gloucester. An exception was Uncle Freddy, an eccentric, who came to Boston to be under the protection and care of my father.

During the reading at the Mount, Wissler mostly asked me to read about my immigrant family. I had planned to read from the rock, jazz, and gonzo pieces. But I was truly surprised by the audience response.

I discovered that ancestry, the stories of immigrants, has a broad appeal. The poems about my family often resonate with readers. It is something that, as a nation of descendants of immigrants, we all share. At least for our generation there is an urge to know who we are and where we come from.

This is not necessarily a concern for the young.

In my family, for example, the descendants of farmers and a bootlegger, or a fruit seller from Brooklyn, went on to become doctors, lawyers, a judge, professors, and graduates of prestigious MBA programs. There is a commonality of prosperity. Perhaps that comes with an indifference to more humble origins.

Mostly I have written to please myself. As I explained to my friend, a therapist, writing family stories has been therapeutic but without the expense. It has been a way of dealing with conflict and becoming more courageous about revealing abuse. The poems have been getting tougher. We talked about who owns our life experience. What happens when what might be told to a therapist or shared with trusted friends becomes material for making art? There is risk and collateral damage.

There is an ever-wider reach as daily life and events, seasons, travel, encounters with musicians and artists have been woven into the tapestry of the work. Given my age there are concerns about mortality, the cosmos, and deity. Poets probe life experience through aesthetic use of language.

Mostly the poems are sharp, focused, and brief. One may sample and reflect. Or turn the page. As Aristotle defined tragedy, the action is confined to a single day. In the case of many of the poems, they were written in a matter of minutes. The epic ones have taken as much as an hour to write but require just minutes to read.

For me that seems total gonzo.

First Use of "Gonzo"

"Pop Music: 25,000 at Stadium Hear Ten Years After"
By Charles Giuliano
Boston Herald Traveler
Friday, July 3, 1970
Section A, Page 9

Some 25,000 gonzo fans jammed the bowl end of Harvard Stadium, Wednesday, July 1 to hear their sex-rock idols, Ten Years After. The Schaefer Festival foams on with top rock.

Plagued by equipment failure, Mott the Hoople, the opening act, was off almost as fast as they went on and spent most of the evening brushing their hair.

Cheering the endless stream of crashers flowing in from the opposite end zone, the kids turned to amusing themselves with wine, chanting, grass and Frisbees. Rockets and firecrackers added to the frenzy. The scene in the stadium was worthy of Caligula.

Milling about during the long break the HT canvassed the ladies: Carol from Canada has never seen Alvin Lee before but has all his records. Pam from Newton was more emphatic, "Wow, I just flipped out on him at the Tea Party."

The men registered lesser emotions. Doug Haley was blasé, "Yeah, sort of, but not terribly huge." While Leonard, from Dartmouth, Mass came all the way to see Alvin. David from Teaneck, N.J. was a touch bitter, "He's just a male sex symbol."

Forty-five minutes later the PA limped back to life and Mott the Hoople back on for a number. Then more intermission while ushers attempted to clear backstage to bring out TYA.

Madhana, a Krishna Consciousness member, saw TYA at Woodstock and liked it then but finds that "The sounds may be terribly pleasing but they are materialistic and everything is temporary. The more you chant the nicer it gets, Hare Krishna."

At 10 p.m. after two hours of wine, reefer and Frisbee, TYA came on. With his red Gibson covered with peace symbol decals slung around his neck, Alvin Lee puffed on a cigarette. Ever-Adonis-like, under a sculpted mop of blonde hair, Alvin wore a flowered cowboy shirt and jeans. From his belt a motel key dangled suggestively.

The opener "Move Like a Mountain" brought surges of recognition. Floating on the rock-solid rhythm of beak-nosed bassist, Leo Lyons, the diminutive organist, Chick Churchill and Alvin's brother Ric on drums, Alvin launched into the furious note clusters which have earned him a rep as the fastest guitarist in rock. It's all in the vibrato, however, which gets more from a chord.

The girls swooned for Alvin's "School Girl" with the suggestive lyrics. Following with "Spoonful" was almost too much. Then Alvin, Chick and Leo went off for a cigarette leaving Ric thumping through the drum vehicle "Hobbit."

Scat singing effectively Alvin twists his jaw and pouts the lyrics through pursed lips mouthing the mike. After the vocal break

Alvin rocks back to trade licks with Leo, humorously parodying the style of Chuck Berry with fake dance steps. TYA is often faulted for not being very original but who cares when they rock through "Sweet Little Sixteen" or "Blue Suede Shoes."

Abandoning the organ, Red Sox shirted, Chick Churchill mounted an amp to lead the audience in a wild clapping finale. And the fans swarmed the car as a police escort drove TYA back to the motel.

Acknowledgments

Like Irish twins *Total Gonzo Poems* is the second book of poetry to be published within a calendar year.

The first volume *Shards of a Life* was launched at Edith Wharton's The Mount on its terrace in June. The successful event was hosted by Susan Wissler its director. A reading at the Williams Faculty Club just five months later included selections from both books.

During the summer there was a reading, arranged by my sister, Pippy Giuliano, at the Annisquam Village Library where I spent my early years. Many old friends and family members attended. I read a number of selections from the series *Nugents of Rockport* which are collected in this second book. For that event Gail McCarthy wrote a wonderful feature story in the *Gloucester Daily Times*.

In May of 2016 Astrid Hiemer and I are invited to a residency at the Gloucester Writer's Center by its director Henry Ferrini. We will both work on projects. My time will be spent for further research of the Nugent family legacy with plans for another publication. I also hope to explore the poet Charles Olson and the literary history of Cape Ann.

Since it was launched through *Berkshire Fine Arts* in August 2014 the poetry project has gained momentum. There were 100 poems in the first book while the second is larger with another 139. Since it went to the designer there are now some 60 more by early November and momentum for yet another book.

The pace has slowed, morphed, and deepened. It would be nice to think that there has been growth and change from the first book to the second and beyond.

This late blooming burst of energy and creativity has only been possible with the support and effort of a superb first team and beyond that the constant feedback of readers and their critical comments posted to the site. The work is being read and responded to.

As always the first responder is Astrid who provides insights and critical comments. There are almost daily dialogues with my consigliere, Robert Henriquez, who has contributed critical essays for both books. He is the true scholar of this work.

Once again Leanne Jewett has taken on the task of editing the books with an overview of all aspects of publication. Amanda Hill has superbly designed these attractive and accessible books.

Mostly this has been great fun. How exciting to have that vintage total gonzo image of me in my Nudie suit at Castle Hill by Steve Nelson with his wife Jan. It is richly vivid testimony to an era of drugs, sex, and rock 'n' roll.

Finally, a tip of the hat to the late Dr. William J. "Bill" Cardoso a friend and rival in all matters gonzo. And to my mentor and patron the Maine farmer, musician, and seer, James Silin "Jimmy Midnight," who was there the night when I first uttered the word "gonzo." I played drums in his Total Gonzo Band, which was brief but iconic.

Gonzo Shine

An Essay by
J.M. Robert Henriquez
Written for *Total Gonzo Poems*
By Charles Giuliano
2015

"A life examined is a life lived."

That was the closing line in my essay for Charles Giuliano's first book of poetry, *Shards of a Life* (2015). Now the shards have been collected, the fog of forgetfulness is dusted away and the raw honesty of a life and art is in full display. Miraculously Giuliano—a prolific poet by all accounts—has done something extraordinary by publishing his second book of new poetry, *Total Gonzo Poems*, in the same calendar year. Two publications and two hundred thirty-nine poems so far, make for a nascent anthology. Once again, the new poems in this ever-growing opus compel us to rethink our engagement with poetry. It is futile to compare

Giuliano to other poets, hoping to find a defining measure for our common life. That's because according to Giuliano's own poetic praxis, resurrecting the various ironies of life can be outrageous fun, which in turn opens the door for him to engage in the blasphemy of serious play. Charles Giuliano, the first gonzo poet of our time, stands to accomplish that with swashbuckling flair. His poetry is direct, brief, and unapologetically in-your-face. It takes courage to blaspheme through one's art, while seeking the absolute truth in one's life. He has realized it with great facility and brevity in both volumes. In Giuliano's case, his poetry and life are true monozygotic twins.

During our frequent angst-ridden musings, Giuliano often speaks of the low-hanging fruits on the tree of life. We revisit those easily accessible moments of past disquietude as we hope to feel catharsis in the clarity they bring to the present. We do it often, mulling over the vicissitudes of our time with complete honesty, without complete understanding of their purpose or cause. Giuliano takes us closer to the middle boughs of the tree in *Total Gonzo Poems*, "picking" and "plucking" middle-hanging fruits at various stages of maturity. These are other moments of larger themes in a life that demand a fair amount of thoughtful self-investigation. One might argue that manipulating the present and having unfettered access to the past provide a better pathway to knowledge and understanding. It's a new way of writing about these existential moments. The interesting thing about Giuliano's poetry is such effort rewards the reader.

In these poems, Giuliano can be relentless with the fast, syncopated rhythm of his language. He urges us on bebopward, with the stark verses in the poem "Up the River," "Demanding you press on / Further, deeper / Up the river / Into the cave / Where we meet." Looking carefully, there are no lurches, pauses, hitches, or dead spots in his language technique. We're paddling with him upriver, matching our strokes to the brisk rhythm and timing of the words, moving seamlessly from one stroke to the other—the gonzo effect in full throttle. All the while, his intention from the beginning was to herd the reader toward a secret, if not hellish, destination of his choosing—the proverbial heart of darkness, "Exploring the horrific / Unknown / Handful of confidantes / Pleased to be among them." It's almost an act of desperation on his part as he declares willfully, "Without mercy / Or remorse."

At first glance the materials of Giuliano's poetry seem narcissistic, even boastfully so. Essentially, he disregards the entire safety net afforded to traditional poetry for the sake of brutal honesty. There is scant humility in his work, and yet he often shows deference to his critics, not because they may be right sometimes, but because Giuliano has to try his hardest not to condescend. It is clear that his art is his domain, and he is the absolute master of that domain.

The subject matter in Giuliano's poetry comes from a variety of occasions and spaces that are themselves a complex geography of places and origins. Genealogy and geography play important roles in the narrative focus of Giuliano's art. That is why the poems reflect his life with such vivid accuracy. The ancestral poems in "The Nugents of Rockport" series move along the migratory axis at the center of the great narratives of "Fabula America." The epic crossings over the "mare libertatis" are often presented as triumphant episodes of the European diaspora. These brave souls were abandoning wretched conditions for something much better. In order to make some sense of the questions of his European origin, Giuliano eschews those entrenched shibboleths for a more direct and less jingoistic narrative. He is fully aware that, for the most part, those voyages were voluntary, and not enforced.

He is also cognizant of the difficulty of relocating one's roots to a new world.

Giuliano certainly makes a case for the gonzo style as a shift from traditional modernity to a more dynamic, if not extreme, modernity. With "Ancestors"—the second of "The Nugents of Rockport" poems—he clearly demonstrates that the conception of extreme scenarios is an intrinsic element of the gonzo genre. The poem begins with an elucidation of cause, "Born during but/ Emigrated after / The Potato Famine." Followed by the extreme scenario of a cleverly constructed taxonomy of matrilineal ancestry, complete with names, dates, and places. In the end, with surprising effect, the poem strikes a hopeful tone:

Nine formed families
Went forth and multiplied
Populating the world
With democrats
Now with prosperity
Likely some Republicans
Saints preserve us

If Rockport of Cape Ann was the place where scions of the Nugent clan relocated the family roots, Annisquam Harbor is the alternate element for Giuliano's most engaging materials. He deftly uses them to construct existential moments that present his own artistic process as a composite of thinking and experiencing.

Giuliano also shows a great deal of diversity in the *Total Gonzo Poems* volume by casting a wider net across the contemporary landscape. As a journalist, he is a fast and accurate writer with a keen eye for details, which serves him well when he ventures outside the walls of the familiar. Giuliano is ready and well equipped for his foray into gonzo poetry—with its particular kind of weirdness. Aside from the ancestral theme of this collection, there are other poems filled with his own insight into how he sees the world. "Birth of Gonzo" is a strong narrative of the style that brings home the matter of rightful ownership of the term "gonzo." There's a wicked sense of humor and moral indignation in the language Giuliano uses in the poem—probably written with both the pen and the sword. The idea of a "proto-gonzo" style emerged from the chrysalis of his literary juvenilia while in college. He later, in 1970, coined the word "gonzo" as an expression and a style. Early on, Giuliano plunged wholeheartedly into the hipster lifestyle. Not many of the tragicomic aspects of his privileged youth were lost on him. His image as a boisterous enfant terrible still stands today.

Giuliano is now a published poet, a polymathic iconoclast with an edgy quality about him. Yet he anxiously harbors doubts about the craft and wisdom of his poetry. Also, he is fully aware of the perils of courting the new. Changing the rules of the game begets an assumption of selfishness and arrogance. Critics, bona fide or faux, will show the sharpness of their fangs.

Reading poetry correctly is to hear two voices, the reader's and that of the poet. It is a synergistic duet played with great effect. Perhaps, with a conscious attempt to attune to this music, we will be able to also hear other voices faintly echoing in our subconscious. These are the voices of memories, near and far, recounting the history of time. The poet writes the words, but the words are theirs.

That is gonzo shine.

Jean Michel Robert Henriquez is a multimedia artist and broadcast media professional who relocated from New York City to the Berkshires. His broadcasting career at the CBS Television Network spanned more than twenty years. Henriquez subsequently worked in integrated advertising (broadcast, online, and print) as a freelance media consultant and art director/producer.

Dad with Josephine and Charles.

Mary Nugent center with women of the clan.

Beaver Dam Farm back in the day.

The young Mary Nugent.

Mary Nugent raised thirteen children.

Mary and Patrick Nugent before she was a widow in 1900.

The young Josephine Flynn.

Young Josephine Nugent later Flynn.

My grandmother Maria Giuliano.

My grandmothers out for a stroll.

Grandmother in later years.

The Flynns stepping out in grand style.

James and Josephine Flynn.

James and Josephine at home.

Mother and grandmother the 1920s.

Dad and his mother and mother-in-law.

My grandmothers vacationing in Gloucester with an unidentified boy.

Class photo Franklin and Marshall College.

Dad as a teenager in Brooklyn.

Dad at the piano.

Dad on a cruise of the Greek Islands.

Mom graduating from High School.

Mom summer at Wheeler's Point.

Mom as an It Girl.

Mom 1920s.

Mom and Dad 1942, Allston, Mass.

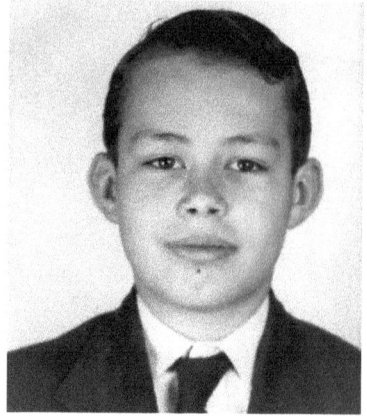

Young Charles.

Dressed for a Bal a Versailles 1950s.

Uncles left to right, Albert, Bill, Dad, and Freddy.

The Flynn Family Christmas 1940s.

Aunt Mary Giuliano.

Young Josephine.

Mom and Josephine.

Josephine and Charles.

Summer in Gloucester.

Charles as a shaver.

Charles and Josephine during a Gloucester summer.

Charles and Malcolm. Photo © 2015
Astrid Hiemer.

The Nugents gathered for a 1980s
reunion in Atlantic City, New Jersey.

Herald Traveler reporters Ian Forman and Charles Giuliano.

Mom and Dad in the 1980s.

At a New York restaurant left to right Esthere Giuliano, Dad, Mom, Nugie, Albert Giuliano and his girlfriend, and Bill Giuliano.

Family gathering left to right, Augusta Henley Cheshire, Josephine Nugent Henley, Michael Moonves, Mom, Dad, Pip, and Josephine.

Crosscurrents

Nugents of Ireland
Not Celtic but Norman
Crossed to England
Not long after 1066
From the village
Nogent in France
First noted AD 930
Hence de Nogent
Chavalier Gilbert de Nogent
Left for Ireland
Some hundred years on
By 1486 Baron Devlin
Then Earl of Westmeath in 1621
Took up the Irish cause
Famous battles
Christopher Nugent at Limerick, 1619
Soldiers with James II in Scotland 1715
Reprisals for backing Stuarts
Land confiscated
Some returned to France
Then the troubles
British rule and famine
Fought the Black and Tans
Dermot (Jeremiah) Nugent and Margaret Power
Raised five
Thomas (b. 1842), Dermot (b. 1844), Margaret (b. 1846), Mary (b. 1846)
The youngest Patrick (b. 1850)
My great grandfather
Then twenty
Seeking a better life
Boarded the steamer Samaria

May 3, 1871
Booked steerage to Boston
East Boston tenement
Sweetheart Mary Donovan
Left April 23, 1872 aboard Siberia
After three years of courting
She demanded his intentions
Honorable Mary he said honorable
But proved not to be
Raising thirteen in Rockport
Dead at 50
Blood poisoning
From treating infected horse
Having spread his seed
Far and wide
America where the blarney
Thrives with Norman woes

The Nugent family crest.

Ancestors

Born during but
Emigrated after
The Potato Famine
Patrick Nugent (1850–1900)
Parish of Ratchcormacho
County of Waterford
Ireland
Mary Josephine Donovan (1851–1927)
Of the old sod
Married in 1875
Farmers settled in Rockport
Leased land
Deep into Dogtown Common
Raised a clan of thirteen
Many hands for honest labor
Charles Nugent (1876–1959)
Starting in right away
Then another a year later
Margaret Josephine (1877–1949)
My grandmother
Followed by more and more
Robert (1879–1913)
John M. (1881–1913)
Two sons deceased in their prime
Just before the Great War
Thomas Francis (1882–1949)
James Paul (1884–1973)
Irish Twins
Henry M. (1886–1966)
William Edward (1886–1974)
Julia M. (1889–1944)

George C. (1890–1965)
Joseph (1891– Unknown)
Mary E. (1893–1913)
Untimely death at twenty
Catherine (1897–Unknown)
The last at 46
Thirteen over 21 years
Three gone too soon
Patrick fathered another
Rogue that he was
By sister-in-law
Great Aunt Caddy without heirs
Nine formed families
Went forth and multiplied
Populating the world
With Democrats
Now with prosperity
Likely some Republicans
Saints preserve us

The Nugent clan and the beginning of the next
generation in Rockport 1920s.

The Gloucester headstone
for Mary and Patrick Nugent.

Patrick Nugent

Indeed a handsome devil
Full of mischief
From a wealthy family
The youngest
Sent packing to America
Met a lovely peasant woman
Just off the boat in Charlestown
What are your intentions
She asked just as Astrid
Did on our first date
Honorable Mary, he said
Honorable
Not known for hard work
Horses and cock fights
Carousing about
Having a grand old time
She with that large family
Kept busy
Dawn to dusk
Working to make a
Go of a fine farm
Everyone but Patrick
Seeing to the chores
During busy summers
Extra hands including
Mary's sister
Patrick in the hay loft
Got her with child
On his death bed asked
Did you love me Mary

Yes Patrick
A love that never
Was returned

Young Patrick Nugent the scion of the clan was not known
for hard work.

Good Harbor Beach

Most who settled
Cape Ann
Toiled the sea
Fishermen of Gloucester
Clusters of homes
Along the shore
Interior vast and empty
Dogtown Common
Later abandoned
Cellar holes and stone walls
All that remains
The Nugents
Patrick and Mary
Immigrants from Ireland
Married in 1875
Rented Beaver Dam Farm
In Rockport
From the Babsons
Until the widowed matriarch
Died in the 1920s
Of the nine children
That survived their thirteen
Most left farming far behind
Migrated away to other
Cities and trades
George bought property
Across the road
Now called Nugent Stretch
Raised pigs and cows
A great wedge of land
Including all of

Good Harbor Beach
View of Twin Lights
Ever more popular
With summer bathers
For decades city
Maintained it then
Sued to own
Dragged on for years
Finally as reported
April 10, 1939
Charlie Nugent
Settled for $35,000
Son of a beach
Now cost fifteen bucks
Just to park
If you can find a space
All that's left
Is the Nugent name
And just a tad of
Gloucester fame

Pig farmer George Nugent was
the Boss Tweed of Gloucester.

Beaver Dam Farm

Gloucester to Rockport
Old Nugent Farm Road
Condos named for them
On land of great-uncle George
Once owned all of
Good Harbor Beach
Boss Tweed of Gloucester
Appointed Mayors
Lost most of his foot
Farm accident
Visited Mom each summer
In posh Annisquam
Old-money Yankees
Where Catholics are rare
What will you have
She would ask
Always whiskey neat
Leaning on his cane
False choppers clanking
Thick accent slurring words
The gift of gab
Full of grand stories
Homestead rented from
Babson family
Some 32 acres
Pasture and gardens
Abandoned in 1927
When the matriarch Mary
Died at 76
Worn out from raising 13
Townies torched house and barn

Just to watch the blaze
Nothing better to do
Old stone kitchen
Dated to 1658
All that survives of
Beaver Dam Farm
George moved up the road
Raising cows and pigs
Where our roots are
Planted in peasant earth

The Nugents rented from the
Babsons from 1875 to the 1920s
when Mary died.

Mary Nugent in front of a farm building that
was torched by vandals in the late 1920s.

What remains of Beaver Dam
Farm is the 17th century stone
kitchen.

Beaver Dam Farm carved into the stone wall.

1913

In old age
Mom looked so like
Her grandmother
Recalled summers
As a child
Spent on Beaver Dam Farm
Hearing the matriarch
Crying herself to sleep
Mourning the loss
Just before the war
Armory Show in New York
Paterson New Jersey Strike
1913 such a terrible year
Death of two oldest sons
Not on Flanders Field
Robert and John
Fatal accidents
Driving the wagon to Gloucester
With shoes to repair
Horse spooked and bolted
Thrown and killed
Like Isadora Duncan
Scarf caught in spokes
Death by motorcycle
Back to back
Then one more
No end of grief
Daughter Mary
Just twenty
Lingering tuberculosis
Mom remembered

Her aunt frail and coughing

Great-grandmother

On her own

After philandering Patrick passed

At just fifty

Running the farm alone

Enduring terrible loss

As the world went to war

Over There

The Nugent clan in front of Beaver Dam Farm in Rockport. Henry of 13 children missing with my mother in front of her grandmother Mary. Circa 1912. Three died in 1913.

James Flynn

The Flynns settled in Canada
Came to Rockport
Masons who worked on
Granite breakwater
Ran inn and tavern
In Annisquam
Then Gloucester
James got drunk as a teenager
Sick as a dog
Swore off booze
Teetotaler
Ran saloons and hotels
In Boston
Silver Dollar Bar
Lower Washington Street
Largest in Boston
Never allowed women
Caused trouble
During prohibition
Bootlegger
Ran whiskey from Canada
Drove a Pierce-Arrow
Loaded for run
Through Smuggler's Notch
In New Hampshire
Mom made deliveries
After school
Knock on the door
From Mr. Flynn
Ran speakeasy
Paid off the cops

Daughter Dorothea
With deceased first wife
Josephine McDougall
Next married Josephine Nugent
They raised Mom, Arthur, Mary, and James
As well as Dorothea
Like her own
Lured away by her aunts
Broke my grandmother's heart
Rarely mentioned after that

The young James Flynn.

Family Business

Tavern in Gloucester
1910 or so
Newlyweds
James Flynn and Josephine Nugent
Of the Rockport clan
They moved running
Bars and hotels in Boston
Theatre district
Brigham's Café
642 Washington Street
Silver Dollar Bar
Largest in the city
Shubert Tap
Next to the theatre
Clam supper
Just seventy-five cents
All the fixings with
Dancing and floor show
No cover charge
Free lunch
Spittoons on the floor
The fighting Irish
Grandma dolled up at night
When he came home
Habit she stuck to
Summers tending to us
Rustic cottage at Red Gates
On Cape Ann
Kerosene stove
Chips from the
Iceman

Block over his back
Brawny fellow
Trailed by kids
Before refrigerators
Ended his rounds
Amazed me after supper
Seeing her all dressed up
Just for us kids
Makeup and perfume
After he was gone
She not that long later
Prohibition era
Running speakeasies
Legit booze
Smuggled from Canada
All good stuff
And kegs of beer
Paying off cops
The Great Depression
Brother can you spare a dime
Democrats for FDR
Two sons and son-in-law
Uncle Jimmy Sullivan
Battle of the Bulge
Helped take Berlin
Arthur later Judge Flynn
Setting up
Clubs for officers
Confiscating wine cellars
Appropriating villas
Running nightclubs

The family business
Uncle Brother
Landing planes
Based in England
Living well
Handsome in a uniform
Last to speak with
Joe Kennedy
Trying to guide him home
Ditched in the Channel
Years later on a plane
Told that to Senator Ted
Memories of
The Greatest Generation
Setting forth
To multiply

The Old Brigham's

DANCING EVERY
EVENING
NO COVER
CHARGE

BANQUET ROOMS
FOR
PRIVATE PARTIES

EAT YE AND DRINK YE MERRILY
FOR TIME HATH WINGS

CAFE AND PALM GARDEN RESTAURANT
JAMES F. FLYNN, PROP.
BRUCE E. RICHARDS, MGR.
FAMOUS FOR FINE FOOD FOR A CENTURY
642 WASHINGTON STREET   BOSTON, MASS.
TELEPHONE HUBBARD 7131

TONIGHT at Brigham's

642 WASHINGTON ST.

Clam Supper

75c

Sweet Mixed Pickles, Clam Chowder, Pilot Bisciuts, Steamed Clams with Broth and Drawn Butter.

FRIED CLAMS

Tartar Sauce, Fr. Fr. Potatoes, Cole Slaw, Ice Cream and Coffee

DANCING & FLOOR SHOW

Establishments owned and managed by my grandfather James Flynn.

Irish Lads

Fit as a fiddle
Fighting Irish
Stout lads
Fine athletes
Three-man bike
The Nugents
Charles and Robert
Brother-in-law
James Flynn
Me grandfather
May 28, 1898
Set world record for mile
One minute and fifty-five
Faded memory
Of blarney burst of speed

The nine sons of Patrick and Mary Nugent with insert of Henry then departed to Vancouver circa 1912.

Baylor Bullies

Columbia School of Pharmacy
Working three jobs
Hard times
Supporting the family
School at night
Dad flunked out
Too exhausted to focus
Decision to study full time
Franklin and Marshall
Lancaster, Pennsylvania
Home for break
Caught 1919 flu
Almost died
Heard funeral bands
Passing by in Brooklyn
Baylor University
For medicine
Long train ride south
Deep in the heart of Texas
No place for Sicilians
Wore letter sweater
With Big B
Hard working and proud
Angered Good Old Boys
Assaulted by crackers
Fellow students
Boxed in self defense
Tough city kid
Put a hurt on them
Never bothered after that
Back to New York

Home to his Mom
Surgery resident
Bellevue Hospital
Promising career
Breaking out of
Poverty

Dad sixth from left in front of frat house at Franklin and Marshall.

On the Porch

Arrogant young surgeon
Swarthy Sicilian
Swept Mom off her feet
Proposed within week
Of first date
Fast marriage
Brief honeymoon
Then drove her back
To hospital dorm
She on ambulance call
First visit as newlyweds
88 Gardner Street, Allston
Up the road from
Old Braves Field
When Boston had two
Major-league teams
On the porch
Grandpa Flynn
Stoic and tight lipped
Only knew what he
Read in the papers
Smoking his pipe
Dad asked
What are you smoking Mr. Flynn
Shared tobacco
Puffing in rockers
Few words said
No need
The peace pipe
For a mixed marriage

Left to Right Charles Giuliano with daughter Josephine, Josephine Flynn, Uncle Brother, Josephine Fynn, Aunt Mary Sullivan holding young Charles.

Dad and Charles.

Flynn family home 88 Gardner Street, Allston, Mass.

Josephine Flynn and her son James (Brother) in Allston.

Visit

Clinton Street, Brooklyn
Doctor's row
Knock on the door
Surprised to see Mr. Flynn
Never before
Left Boston
Came by train
To see Doc
Only one he trusted
Terrible case of
Hemorrhoids
Dad recalled
Fixing him up in the office
Big as ripe grapes
Snipped and sutured
Old man puffing on his pipe
Bond of love
Worth all the pain
Stayed to visit
The World Fair
Back home
Wrote a rare letter

Letter 1940

From James Flynn to Dr. Charles Giuliano the day after birth of
Charles, Jr. on October 25, 1940

Boston, Oct. 26

To My Dear Son Charles,

The Dock 3 am. I have been thinking since you telephoned about
everything.
Well you know I was worried this time I can't tell you why but I was.

Let's hope everything is O.K. now.

Charles Jr. I hope a doctor sure. Well let's hope they Boy & Girl are
as bad and good as their Farther and Mother. I wouldn't give a
cent for them if they wasent as bad and I know they have a tuff
job to bee better.

They have a good Mother and Farther to set the example. What
a foundation for two children. All I hope for is their health the
carietor will develop as they grow. Missies smartness and two years
will bee a great advantage to the boy. An older sister is a great
advantage to any boy. Helps to keep them straite.

I hope Joe will take it eaisey now don't hurry. I am wondering most
how Missie will take it. Don't you and Joe every think anybodys
success let temhave the manchons and solutude you have the
children. I know where they will be another happy Old Man. To
bad someone else couldnt share the happiness with him.

Dock I never visited anybody in my life only you and Joe. I would rather go to 294 Clinton St. than the Worlds Fair. Dock I owe no man in the world only you.

All I ask is my health and a little luck so that I may pay back my appreciation. I won't die happy until then.

Charles the people at home are more proued of they way I got the suit than they are of the suit itself. The McDevetts thaught it was auftel thoughtful of you. Whitch I was glad to bost about.

Remember me to the Ruffalos. May all your people kiss Joe and Missie for me Charles Jr and God Bless you Charles.

Jim Flynn

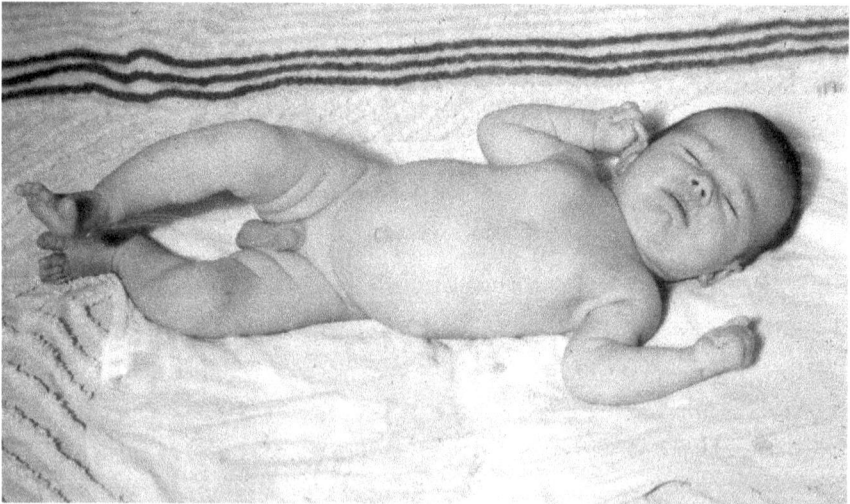

The infanta Charles II.

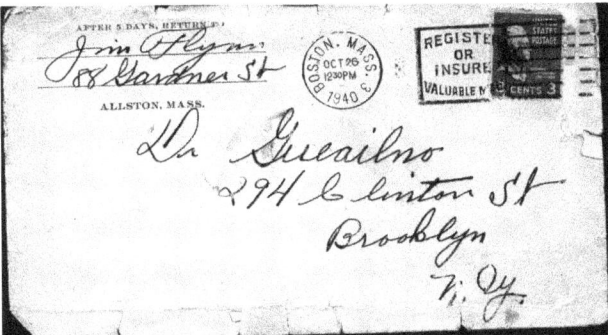

Letter from my grandfather James Flynn the day after I was born.

Sweet Dreams

Now I lay me down to sleep
Prayers at bedtime
Mom tucking me in
Secrets and confessions
Like the nuns taught me
Initially
Will you marry me when I grow up
Wait for me
We'll see she said softly
Later an update
Wedding cancelled
Tearfully
Don't know how to tell you
Hope you're not mad
I want to be a priest
The sisters say
Best you can do with your life
Serve Jesus
Like they do
Calmly responded
It's a calling
If that's what you want
After seeing Swan Lake
The old Boston Opera House
Decided to be
A ballerina
Or maybe a cowboy

Charles as a child.

Garden of Eden

Spring Garden Show
Mechanic's Hall
Huntington Ave
Long gone
Mom took us
Spectacular displays
All in bloom
Even a real waterfall
Fragrance in the air
Peasant roots
Irish potato planters
Fled the famine
Settled in Rockport
Beaver Dam Farm
Other side Sicilian
Dirt under fingernails
Urge to grow
From seeds
Visions of summer
Vegetables and gourds
Bought all kinds
For Annisquam
Where to plant
First-ever garden
Wanted middle of
Backyard
Full sun
Mom said no
Pointed to the woods
Cleared a patch
Surrounded by shrubs

Six-feet-square
Rows of
Corn, radishes, gourds, carrots, lettuce
Everything stunted
Mini-ears of blighted corn
Radishes more or less OK
Grandpa Nano visited
Proud to show him
No sun he said
No sun no grow
Kneeling on the ground
With pocket knife
Transferred lettuces
To sliver of light
Lesson learned
Still trying to
Grow vegetables

Trim

Lazy days of summer
Norwood Heights
Posh Annisquam
Neighbor Mr. Bishop
Asked Dad about
Hiring me to paint trim
Big shingle-style house
On a high ladder
Baking in the sun
Meticulous work
Careful and patient
A week of hard labor
Money to take
Lisa to the movies
Went to collect my pay
He was on the phone
Too busy to deal with me
Waited then finally
Let's see that's
Seventy-five cents an hour
Times eight per day
That comes to
He pulled small change
From his pocket
I said nothing and left
Monday passed
Then Tuesday
That weekend he
Spoke to my dad
Who asked me why

I quit a good job
Not worth it for
Chump change
Damn Yankees

Son et Lumière

Midnight
After supper in the Orangerie
Bal a Versailles
Would have preferred
Hall of Mirrors
Evoking the Sun King
Stepped out on the terrace
For traditional
Son et Lumière
Fireworks
French horns from the woods
Little sister Pip
Wearing crown jewels
Necklace of
Champagne corks
Collected at many
Regal receptions
So clever and inventive
Mocking with panache
Event that Josephine
The debutante
Took to heart
After the bal
Hitched a ride
Back to Paris
Limo of Pittsburgh heiress
Stopped for
Onion soup in
Les Halles
Wearing formal attire
Like a photo spread
In Vogue

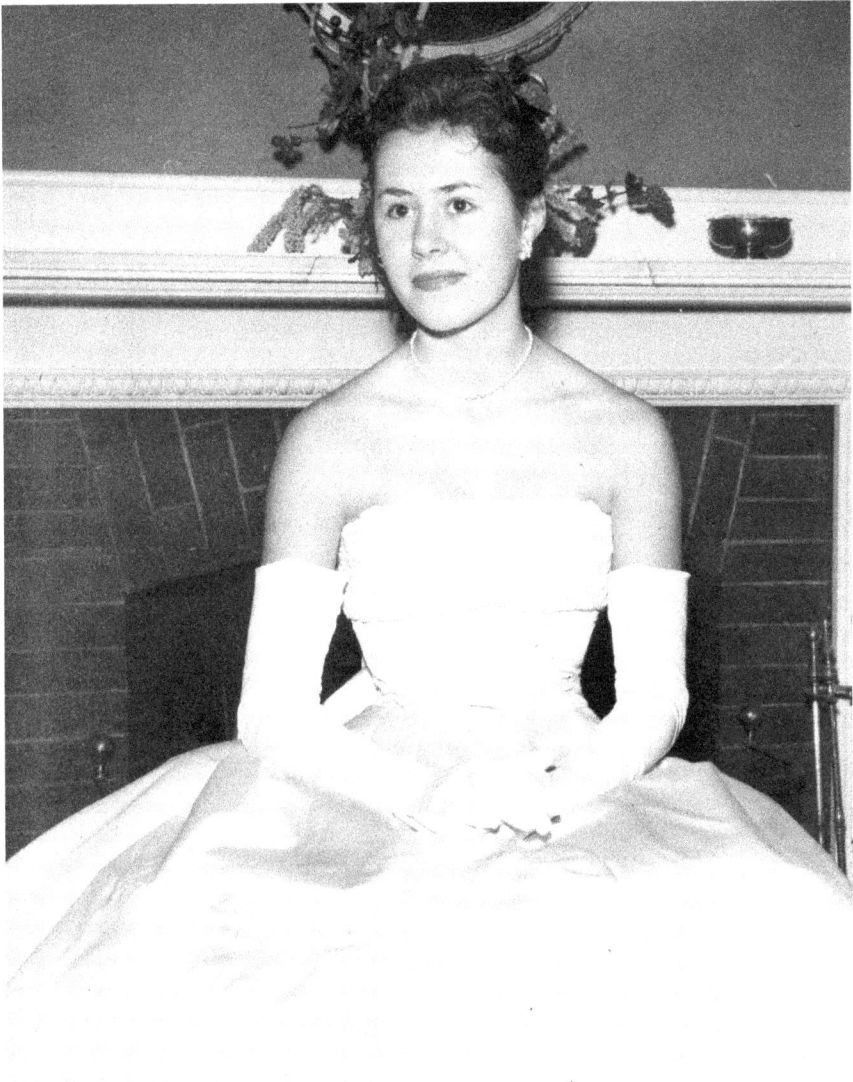

Josephine as a debutante.

Bouillabaisse

From Nice
Rented small car
Stick shift
Unlike Dad's Cadillac
We had to push it
Backing up
Meandering along
Riviera
Turned off at
Villefranche-sur-Mer
Tiny, quaint
Village by the sea
Still vivid
Half century later
Rustic restaurant
Edge of the harbor
Specialty of the house
Bouillabaisse
Rich stock
Brimming with fish
Stained yellow with saffron
Lots of prawns
Piping hot
Scorching to
Our American taste
Too much so
Abandoned
Perhaps wisely
Wildly enthusiastic
The True Sicilian
Devoured his

Then ours
Next few days
Payback
Twice burned
Torched esophagus
Utter agony
Many times since
Ordered the dish
Always disappointing
Toned down
Never again authentic
That scorching village soup
So long ago

Cancer

At the drawing table
Working on watercolors
Large and colorful
Wasted for inspiration
Evoking the muse
Glanced at elbows
Black as night
Tangerine textured
Panicked
Cancer of the elbows
Possible double
Amputation
Called Mom
Dr. Flynn
Quavering voice
Described symptoms
Listened then said
Dramatic pause
Wash them
Dust from graphite
Instantly
Cured

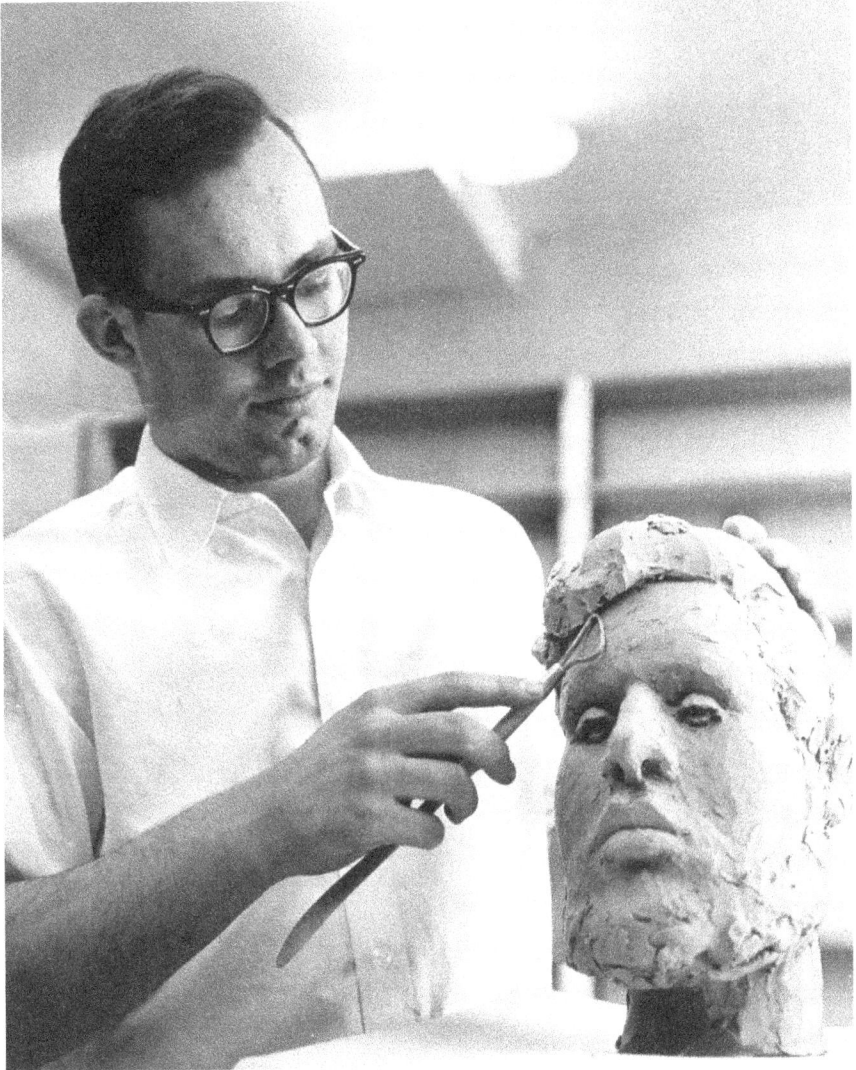

Sculpting at Brandeis.

Pippy

Mom got real fat
Huge bloated belly
Thought she was sick
Needed her tummy tapped
Dad woke Jo and me
April 5, 1949
You have a new sister
How did it happen
That summer
Older girl
At Lighthouse Beach
Explained
First viewing Pip
Asked what I thought
Looks like a fish
Living doll
Plaything
Mean older brother
It slipped
Got over that
During family gatherings
With cousin Ellen
Examined Dennis
Their patient
In Mom's office
Cambridge neighbors
Dinner once a week
Pesto and pasta
Frequent date
Covering rock concerts
Crush on singer Peter Wolf

Lived in my building
Peter this is Pip
Pip this is Peter
Years in the Orient
Buddhist vegetarian
Infuriated Dad
His little girl
Finding her way
Married Yuri
Had Sarah the sailor
Another life with the
Russians
Global travel
Recently Cambodia
Staying in touch
Lots of laughs
Deep discussions
Best friends
For life

Class photo of Pip,
Beaver Country Day School.

Pip as a ballet student.

Let Her Eat Cake

At Brandeis
Cholmondeley's Coffee House
In the Castle
Where Mom attended med school
Before it was Brandeis
Entertainment
On weekends
Folkies like
Mitch Greenhill
Jackie Washington
Even the legendary
Lightning Hopkins
Invited sister Pip
Nine years younger
Now no big deal
Then huge difference
A decade later
Often my date
Covering rock and jazz
Best friends
Weekly dinners
The squirt was thrilled
Then it happened
The waitress came
I ordered modestly
Within my means
She asked for cake
Miffed I said
You had to order the cake
Later a running gag
Reminded of her generosity

So many loans
From her allowance
Never paid back
What a bounder
Recently dinner at the Club
Elegant setting
Spouses Yuri and Astrid
Four of us
Visiting Boston
Told her
Pip you can have the cake
We laughed
Now that I
Can afford it

Brother and sister hanging out.

Lotus

Always frugal
Good for a loan
Rarely paid back
Lifetime of indebtedness
On every level
Daddy's little girl
The late love child
After two failures
Jo and me
Threatened detectives
To watch her in Wisconsin
Great escape
Finishing degree
After Pine Manor
Furtive first sex
Looking over her shoulder
Or out the window
For them
The fearful shadows
Back home
Worked for the phone company
Long enough
Saving money to leave
For Japan
Then on to Thailand
Trek in Cambodia
Ancient temples
Seemingly forever
In exchanges of letters
Afraid of losing her
Eventually returned

Buddhist vegetarian
Tears at Thanksgiving
Refused turkey
Dad flung on her plate
The drumstick
Just to look at it
Like normal Sicilians
Carnivores
Furious at her defiance
By then
He lost her
In meditative silence

Mary Louise Giuliano as a teenager.

Pesto

Neighbors in Cambridge
Before husband Yuri
Sister Pip best friend
Me in the Murder Building
Short walk from
Memorial Drive condo
Weekly dinners
Indian Restaurant in Central Square
Young and Yees on Church Street
He chuckled when seating us
Cheap mediocre Chinese food
Or cooking at home
Weekly invitation
Not always willing
Too tired she said
A magic word
Pesto
The clincher
Sure be right over
Then as always after
The meal
Was it good
Did you like it
Was it really good
Wearing her down
Me so needy
Eventually
Reluctant affirmation
Pip
Do Curly
From the Three Stooges

Pleading
Just to shut me up
She did it so divinely
That growling sound
Fingers snapping just right
The final fluttering hand
Then
Oh Pip do it again
Please
Come on do Curly
Big brothers
Can be such a pain
So she got
Married

A glamour shot of Pip.

Irish Spring

Damp spring weekends
Summer house in Annisquam
Tweaking the seasons
Roaring fire
Shots of Southern Comfort
To kill the chill
Deep in your bones
Walks to the ominous beach
Deserted of bathers
Playing canasta and monopoly
Simple Saturday suppers
Franks and beans
Brown bread
Grilled with butter
Lots of ketchup and mustard
To bed with clammy sheets
Shiver till you sleep
Now and then
Mom's favorite
A lovely boiled dinner
Corned beef
Cabbage and potatoes
All in one pot
Her best cooking
Sad to say
Today we had it for lunch
Served in every bar in America
Irish or not
Remembering me mum
On Paddy's Day

Bris

We lived in Brookline
A Jewish community
Warm spring day
A Sunday
After morning mass
Not normal office hours
The parents seated on the porch
Dad insisted I watch
A circumcision
By a goy doctor
Mom helping
Instead of the mohel
Clamp circling foreskin
Gently tightened
Ring of red
The infant howled
Ritual pain
Abraham's covenant
Sent me bolting
Out into warm sun
Barfing all over
Surging empathy
For the kid
Still have mine

Samson

Toke in the backyard
Good buzz
The family Steinway upright
Improv
Moved by the muse
Evoking Monk and Tristano
In a groove
Eyes closed
Feeling the funk
Chunky Monky chords
Ersatz flashy runs
Mom crept up
Armed with scissors
Quick as a wink
Hacked off
Hunks of hair
Ruined my
Hipster image
Moms have a way
Of bringing us
Back to earth
Where blues
Don't shine

Photo collage of Mom in Annisquam by Charles Giuliano

Uncles

In Brooklyn
Sicilian immigrants
Andrew and Maria
Raised eight
Children of
Fruit seller
Four boys
Charles the oldest
Albert, Bill, and Freddy
The girls
Rose, Catherine, Mary,
Stella
Butchered by a surgeon
Removing tonsils
Slit her throat
In their kitchen
Then asked for next
Victim for slaughter
As Dad, later a surgeon
Recalled with disgust
Knew my uncles
Holiday visits
Summers in Gloucester
And Mary first a nurse
Then early flight attendant
For Pan Am
Dad a doctor
Bill a PhD in Romance Languages
Handsome and elegant
Soft of tongue
Light on his feet

Albert dropped out
To marry Olga
Freddy cut loose
The youngest a bohemian
Regret not having more contact
Grew up with the Irish
Who thought we were foreigners

Dad at the wedding of his
brother Albert and Olga.

Dad in Gloucester with uncles
Bill, left, and Albert.

My grandfather Andrew Giuliano, left, with associates in their Brooklyn market.

Uncle Freddy

Card Carrying Commie
Proud of it
Depression years
During day gig
Chatting with co-worker
Comrade and red
Disdained a nearby
Lumpen prol
Freddy said
Everyone's interesting
For some reason
Called him over
Discussed his hobby
Raising pigeons
On the roof
Like Brando in
On the Waterfront
Came to work
The next day
A bird in his shirt
Beaming for his friends
Tossed it out the window
It will be home
Waiting for me
When I get there
He said proudly
With nothing to lose
But his chains

Uncle Freddy was an actor during the WPA.

Freddy sailing for England.

Freddy left and Dad riding horses in Central Park.

Freddy's Music Unlimited

Fourth son
Youngest of eight
Bohemian and eccentric
Handsome when young
Actor during the WPA
Eva Le Gallienne's company
Crime and Punishment
On Broadway
Loved all things Russian
Particularly Dostoyevsky
Always had a book
Shoved in his pocket
Wild youth
Laughed that his pooch
Goofy knew
Running ahead off the leash
All the watering holes
With handsome patron
Sailed to Europe
Later breakdown
Under Dad's care
Moved to lower end of
Beacon Hill
Opened record shop
Freddy's Music Unlimited
In Newton Corner
Worked for him on Saturdays
Drove in his Renault
Picking up product
Small and easy to park
Tried to clean the shop

Displays out of season
RCA dog out front
Promo item stolen
Early TV in window
Drew crowds at night
Back then you listened
Before buying
Playing Sinatra's
Young at Heart
First jazz albums for Christmas
Duke and Satchmo
Wore the grooves out
Store closed
All those music shops
Wiped out
By wholesalers
Joined a union
Proofreader for newspapers
Told me
Tough talk
If you want to be an artist
Learn a trade

Twilight of the Don

Surgeon's last celebration
Gravely ill
Bravely facing it
First of September
Turning eighty
Also celebrating hers
Troubled granddaughter
Seasonal illness
Summer becomes fall
When others
Return to work and school
No more easy days
On the beach
He so proud and controlling
With no power over her
Spinning out of control
Chronic headaches
Dominating the room
Passively from the couch
Stoic at the head of the table
Where once he ruled
Family gathered
Doomed celebration
Candles on the cake
Gathering last breath
She smashed it
Frosting on fist
Wrestled
Held down
Screaming in rage
He rigid and silent
Dead by New Year

Dad taking swings into the unknown.

Father's Day

Fathers are supposed to
Teach their sons
How to do stuff
Fix things
Like cars and appliances
Carpentry and basic plumbing
Handyman skills
When something went wrong
Dad called an electrician
To change a lightbulb
Workers to do this and that
Paid them and said
Have a cigar
We played catch
A few times
In the backyard
Went to some boxing matches
His passion
Gillette Friday Night Fights
On TV
At most one or two
Baseball games
So basically
I don't know how to do
Anything but cook and garden
He served family recipes
Amazing meals
Took all day and every pot
Often starting the night before
With Italian Wedding Soup
But didn't garden

That I got from my Sicilian
And Irish heritage
Peasants on both sides
When I got old enough
He wanted to teach me
How to operate
Cure patients of cancer
That kind of thing
Made me watch
Puked and passed out
Can't do anything useful
Except write poems
Like this one
Which is OK I guess
But it would be great
To know how to
Actually fix something

Dad a young doctor with a patient and nurse.

On the Road

Just after the semester
Each year
Flew to Palm Beach
Packed up Mom's car
Driving her home
For summer in Annisquam
Such fun to travel with
What a sport
Best hotels and restaurants
Each year planning itinerary
Williamsburg and Monticello
Sea Islands, Georgia
Wonderful ante bellum Savannah
Charleston, Richmond, Philadelphia
St. Augustine and Daytona with friends
Hours of driving
Off the road chasing barbecue
Great adventures
Never straight through
A week at least
Checking in each night
Down the hall for ice
Bar's open
Martinis and a dividend
Then off for dinner
Long days in the car
Boring cracker radio
One year brought tape recorder
Asked about her life
Nugent family history
The good stuff

Turn off that damned thing
Delving ever deeper
Dark secrets revealed
After lunch
Play it back for me
Pillow on her lap
Fingers twiddling
Listened attentively
Can't find the tapes
Still remember though
Tales of our colorful clan
And map to
Buried skeletons

The Yacht Club House, Annisquam, Mass.

Annisquam Yacht Club.

Spotty

Years of hard work
The Sullivans
Jimmy and Mary
Cousins Susan, Ellen, and Dennis
Moved from Cambridge
To upscale Belmont
A fine home
And their beagle Spotty
They were proud of the mutt
Up the street from
Aunt Caddy
By then a doddering widow
Husband George
Retired from Musicians Union
Vice President
She would cook us a lovely dinner
White on white
Potato, squash, turnips
All mashed and bland
With ham
George had a bar
Real one with stools
In the basement
Told the same stories
Of WWI playing
Drums in the Navy Band
Over there
All seemed copasetic
Sullivans would drop by
With Spotty
Caddy would feed him
Lovely snack

Better than dog food
Served at home
Out of a can
Spotty became a regular
After breakfast
Came by for his snack
Eventually never went back
Moved in with Caddy
Doting on him
Smart dog
The Sullivans were furious
Blood feud
Caddy a little old lady
Not a mean bone
No malicious intent
Spotty was the traitor
Benedict Arnold of dogs
Caddy died
Clearing out the house
On the sly
Uncle Jimmy explored the garage
Could use some tools
Garden hose
Pay back
Evening the score
Closed the garage door
Slamming it shut
Clipped off the tip
Of a finger
Such irony
The curse of Spotty

Astrid

Astrid in Venice on a rainy day.

Fireworks

After the opening
Gallery Naga
Dinner on Newbury Street
Montano's
Long since closed
Some twenty years ago
First date
Red-haired Astrid
Evoking crush on Maureen O'Hara
Met at MIT
Administrator for CAVS
Under Otto Piene
What did you have in mind
She asked
Over pasta
Getting to the point
A relationship
Blurted out
Taken aback
With anyone in mind
Flabbergasted
Possibly mumbling
With you perhaps
There it was out of the bag
Strategy and cover blown
Casanova outed
Ma in Ispagna son già mille e tre
Chimed in Leporello
Walking to the subway
Her idea
Through the Gardens

Park Street
On a bench
Soft rain
Fourth of July
Homeless guys
Lighting firecrackers
Sparklers fizzing
Gentle first kiss
She took the train
To Weymouthport
Next few months
Cloud nine
Still floating

Young Astrid Hiemer.

Kerouac

Not long after we met
Spring break
Hotel in Barcelona
Off La Rambla
Flowers and birds
Middle of avenue
To the sea
Tiny room
Small window
Stood on chair
Looking out
View of elevator shaft
Reading intently
On the Road
Car stuck in the desert
Hudson Hornet
Southwest
Sal looked up
That big sky
All those stars
Empty vastness
Beyond comprehension
Canopy over America
Moved to tears
Solitary sobbing
What Capote called
Not writing but typing
On one big roll
Wire service
Two copies with
Carbon in between

Just kept going
No going back
Furious speed
Feverish inspiration
Words racing on the page
That intensity
So riveting
Alone that night
In Spain
So far from Astrid
Called next day
Just to hear her voice
Passing the desk
Here is your bill señor
Yikes so expensive
After that
Post cards
Sent every day
Jack was my
Travel companion
Muse and champion

Astrid on the roof of the Milan Cathedral

Under the Apple Tree

East Boston
Backyard
Narrow and long
Our pride and joy
Wedding
Under the apple tree
Unitarian minister
Ralph Galen
Stuck in traffic
So he claimed
Wicked late
While we waited
Mom arrived
Two hours early
Astrid not ready
Still cleaning
Daughter Olivia and
Son-in-law Ed
Put to work
Food catered by
Chef neighbor Ritchie
As usual for parties
That morning
I made lasagna
Hot September day
Sweating in suit
Staying relatively calm
Read vows she handed me
No idea what I said
Roasted by Steve
The best man

Followed by toast
More barbs from Pip
What a trip
Are they married yet
Mom asked
Tired of explaining that
Bachelor son
In his fifties
Wasn't gay
Students hired to serve
Never put food in the oven
Too busy enjoying the party
Meanwhile I turned
Water into wine
Served the still-hot
Lasagna
We cut the cake
Exhausted
Back to work
Monday morning
Eventual honeymoon
When we
Found the time

Cake

Visiting friends in Newton
Jay and Tanaaz
From the freezer
To share with them
Top tier of
Our wedding cake
Remembering the
Ceremony under the
Apple tree
Hot September day
In East Boston
Slices of love
Said to
Bring good luck

Oceans

Creatures of the watery world
Coming from the sea
Eons ago
Fish crawling onto land
Learning to breathe
Eventually stand
Killing for food
Then each other
For greed
And pleasure
The ocean is in us
Our warm blood
Saline solution
Urge to return
Primal flow
The watery depths
Surging within
Walking the beach
Joy on her face
Astrid who grew up
Near the Elbe
Breathing the briny air
Seemingly never
More at peace
The wonder of my wife
The Hiemer of my life

Trees

Tight schedule
Walking to
New Orleans Museum of Art
Lost Astrid
Wandered off to shoot a tree
Ancient one
Spanish moss
Small palm
Growing out of it
Come on
No time
I love to photograph trees
It's my art form
Who do you love more
Me
Or Trees
What will it be
She laughed
At the absurdity

Astrid photographing.

Astrid with former MIT/ CAVS fellow Nam June Paik.

Astrid with singer Rita Coolidge.

Friends

Phil's daughter and Baywatch star Jasmine Bleeth with Hoey. Giuliano photo.

Amigos

Marooned in the Berkshires
Outcasts
From other lives in
Major cities
Bigger ponds with larger fish
Sharks
Here now scaled-down to
Swimming with minnows
Nipping at our heels
Not sucking up to
Perceived royalty
Circles of insiders
By birth and privilege
Hard-earned credentials
Not recognized
Musical chairs
Few seats at the table
Memories of
Coffee Corner
Studio visits from Clem
Wearing fine cut British suits
At CBS
Chats about tailoring
Belt or suspenders
Elevator rides with Dan Rather
Globe trotting
Michelin restaurants
On the expense account
Not taking it sitting down
Wit and wisdom
Kicking back

Tit for tat
Take that
Scaramouch
Mark of Zorro
Carved into foreheads
Courtiers and pretenders
Who was that masked man
Kemosabe

Mentor and friend Robert Henriquez.

The G

That night
With poet Rene Ricard
On the town
Ended at the
Balloon Farm
St. Mark's Place
Exploding Plastic Inevitable
Velvet Underground
Gerard doing his whip dance
Lou and Nico
G published a book
On Velvets
Volumes of poetry
Nights at Max's
Backroom with Andy
Under the fluorescent Flavin
Candy Darling vamping
Rene dancing on tables
Tight in leather pants
Later at Benno's
In the Berkshires
Don Snyder took photo
Me and the G
Wearing multiple ties
Endless interviews
First one
Round the clock in NY
Cover of Art New England
Recently discussed
Julia the mother of Andy
About a show at Williams

Living in Hudson
So near yet far
With books and archives
We chat now and then
Working on his memoirs
Factory days
Art and poetry
How those leather pants
Don't fit no more

Poet Gerard Malanga and Asako. Giuliano photo 2015.

Alice's Breast Flaunt

Everyone thought
I wrote that outrageous
Satire in trashy magazine
Alice's Breast Flaunt
Not me
I'm in her cookbook
Chapter on stuffing
Apple in my mouth
Benno took the pictures
Crashing at Jim's pad
Sure but
You'll be sleeping with
My friend Alice
Taking a break from Ray
And the Berkshires
No funny stuff she said
Slipping in beside her
Later stayed at The Church
In the bell tower
Rang in the morning
Not a call to prayer
Thanksgiving feast
Rope over the nave
Ray and the gang
Swinging like Tarzan
My turn on the scaffolding
Looked around
Grabbed the rope
Dropped like a stone
Crashed into the buffet
Huge table of food

Sent the turkey flying
Anniversary planned for August
At The Church
Now the Guthrie Center
Told Benno
I'll pass on the rope
Smiling he said
That's why
We took it down
Alice wrote from P'Town
Am I in your book
Now you are
Next one

Not Plain Jane

Originally a poet
Taught English
Lexington High School
The gnome
Barry Savenor
Among her students
Rafe Jenanian
Colleague
Lived in his mother's home
South End Arabs
Transgendered Frannie
What a piece of work
Also a tenant
With Hal
Studio Coalition
Started in her living room
Hung out
Oldest surviving friend
Went to rock concerts
Stones at the Garden
Sat with Hells Angels
Grateful Dead at BU gym
Burned checks
Forty years and no sense
Moosh Magique
Dancing in the embers
Left all that behind
Reborn as punk rocker
The Rentals
Pseudo Carol on drums
Opened for the Clash

In Harvard Square
Cut Indy records
Cult classics
Round the world
Sang
Gertrude Stein, Gertrude Stein, Gertrude Stein
My favorite song
Atlantic Gallery
Hudson doesn't want to
Talk about it
Always a bit odd
Jeff and Jane
Played Mass MoCA
Have covered her gigs
For decades
Still gives me advice
Mother hen
Oh Charlie, Charlie, Charlie
Yes Jane
Now, like Alice
You're in the book
Next one

Touch of the Poet

Holding court last night
Gallery 51
Two artists and two poets
From a wheelchair
My friend
Stephen Rifkin
Heavily wrapped foot
Propped on a chair
Elevated as he put it
Smashed up
Real bad a couple of
Weeks ago
Car totaled in the woods
Saved by air bags
Taking months to heal
Graphic details
Crawling up and down stairs
Comments on aging
Need to live on one floor
All of us cutting back
More or less
Practiced the exclusive
Poet's grip
Secret handshake
Fraternity of verse
Gave him my book
Signed and inscribed
Sharing a love
Words about words
Next to him
A stack of his books

Sold a couple he said
Took photos
Foot in foreground
Sharp perspective
Like stigmata
Mantegna's
Dead Christ
More mishap
Than martyr

Poet Stephen Rifkin. Photo © 2015 Charles Giuliano.

Martin Mugar

My artist friend
Martin Mugar
Yale BA and MFA
Is wicked smart
Heavy-duty thinker
Creates
Deliciously textured paintings
Candy colors you want to lick
First evening
Elegant Algonquin Club
Commonwealth Avenue
So much to discuss
Such a lively mind
Lingering over dinner
Last guests
Tactfully induced to leave
Suave maître d'hôtel
Bribe of brandy
For the lounge
Moved on to
Boylston Street
Stayed for last call
Pour House
Debating the Fine Arts
Ever since

The artist and theorist Martin Mugar.

Geoffrey

Lunch break
Annisquam Yacht Club
Junior Program
Camp
Sailing, swimming, tennis
Geoffrey cavorting
In front of the TV
Elvis
Blue Hawaii
Doing a hula
Towel as grass skirt
Flowing hands
Like surfing waves
Decades later
On the porch of the Brynmere
Catching up
More sedate
Urbane and accomplished
Loose pants with suspenders
No longer the hellion
I knew and feared
Truly a wild child
Not in his opinion
He thought the same of me
Sharing commonality
Gave me his book of collected verse
Come August I'll hand him mine
Reading them again
So changed
By my book
Ten months later

Start to finish

Team effort

Incredible support

It takes a village

Including his advice

Better understanding

Knowing what it takes

Esoteric confraternity

Published poets

Audience for each other

Private club

No rules or dues

But a secret grip

The clincher

Annisquam poet Geoffrey Movius. Photo © 2015 Charles Giuliano.

Smoki Bacon

Smoki always reminded me
A goombah
Grew up Italian
Brookline Village
Married a Brahmin
Ed Bacon
Hence
The amazing handle
Smoki Bacon
Brightest most sparkling
Hostess with mostest
Ed was a great guy
Kindah quiet and stoic
They hosted annual open house
Fairfield Street
Traditional Back Bay
Pre-condo
Launched the social season
Right after Labor Day
Everyone was there
All factions of the city
Proper Bostonians
Journalists and politicians
Debutantes with playboys
Arts and culture
Do you know
Have you met
She would say
Working the rooms
As I told her
Evoking a hearty laugh

If death walked in
Smoki would say
Death this is Charles Giuliano
Charles Giuliano have you met death

Socialite and arts journalist Smoki Bacon. Photo © 2015 Charles Giuliano.

Consigliere

We never have
Ordinary conversations
On North Street
Strolling after lunch
With Robert Henriquez
Recalling my stating
Basta to easy art
No more room for it
In my heart
Reverberating
No small talk
Annual winter seminars
Burning stacks of CDs
Traditional jazz
New Orleans
Louis Armstrong and Jelly Roll Morton
Next season
Reading Blues People
The avant-garde
Cecil Taylor, Archie Shepp, Sun Ra
Coltrane and Miles
Everest as Kind of Blue
The great ladies
Billie Holiday, Anita O'Day, Blossom Dearie
Mostly he flipped over
Yma Sumac
Listened to her as teenager
In Haiti
Significance of not growing
Up with heritage of slavery
First great liberation

From Colonialism
Toussaint Louverture
Defeating Napoleon
Playing in the palace
'Papa Doc' Duvalier
Later escape to U.S.A.
Legendary ancestor
Hero of Olympics
Racism in America
No dog in the hunt
More recently
Post gonzo and language poetry
Always digging deeper
True North
Compass of explorations
The wild inner
Terra incognita
Life of the mind
Humbled by
Time and flesh
Infinite distances
Of space

Tampa

During drive to
Mardi Gras
Visiting Phil Bleeth
He glad to see us
She not
Corinna full-blown pregnant
Once sleek Moroccan model
About to pop
With Jasmine
Expected baby
Later Baywatch babe
All-you-can-eat fish fry
In Clearwater
That night
Tampa
James Brown in a gym
Basketball court
Jammed
Families with picnic baskets
Nowhere to run
Climbed a
TV camera platform
Amazingly
Dragged her up
Please, Please, Please
Cape bit
Best dancer ever
Spins and splits
Driving that band
Human sea of gyrations
Real down-home

Heat of the night
Outah sight

Phil Bleeth now lives in Thailand. Photo © 2015 Charles Giuliano.

Music

Frank Sinatra performing in Boston. Photo © 2015 Charles Giuliano.

Diana Ross

Long after the Supremes
Going solo
Diana Ross
Concerts on the Common
Facing Boylston Street
Vamping through the hits
Past prime
Looking good
Sleek and elegant
Baby-faced
Fine-boned features
Mane of hair
Descended
Reaching into the audience
Up close and personal
Thrills and chills
Smiles for
A summer night

Diana Ross on Boston Common. Photo © 2015 Charles Giuliano.

Sexual Healing

On Boston Common
Summer series
Strutting the stage
Soul Brother
Marvin Gaye
Paramilitary regalia
Parody of militarism
What's Going On
Voodoo Mojo
Working it
Motown medley
Greatest hits
Masterful performance
Ever more frenzied
Cresting with
Sexual Healing
Ripping off clothes
Down to skivvies
Nearly full monty
That April
Monster unleashed
Father shot him
Stone cold dead

Marvin Gaye in one of his final performances before he was killed by his father.
Photo © 2015 Charles Giuliano.

Tommy

Buddy Ronnie
Hey man
How about The Who
Solid
Dropped windowpane
His treat
Mood enhancer
Gig at
Comm Ave Armory
They did Tommy
In its entirety
Press seats
Front row center
Looking straight up
Who knew
Blown away
Roger in fringed leather
Bare-chested sweating
Mini Adonis
Twirling the mike
Sweeping circles
See me, feel me, touch me
Pete leaping
Helicopter swipes
Bashing at the ax
We looked at each other
Whoosh, wow, wiggy
Like Robert Duval's choppers
In Apocalypse Now
Charlie don't surf
Entwistle the Ox

Stolid bass foundation
For that mayhem
Keith Moon spraying sticks
Sinking into our seats
Pete's ritual
Smashing the guitar
Moon trashing the drums
No encores
Bracing against
Tsunami roaring past
Pinned by the wizard
Having a silver ball

Miles

First question
Months of research
All those albums
What was it like
To play with Bird
Shhheeeeeeetttt
Muthafuggah
Such a drag to
Talk about the past
Flustered
Strategy abandoned
Pen and pad in hand
Eager young critic
What do you want to talk about
Drop back and punt
Were you at the gig tonight
I got a problem
You can help me
Did you hear Keith and Chick
Can't carry them both
Who should I get rid of
Floored
Guess I don't know Miles
They're both great
Playing the Fender electrics
That he liked after
Bitch's Brew
Then a pause
Thinking it over
I'm keeping Keith
He gives me more

Chick sent packing
That night before
Return to Forever
Today I would say
Corea the better choice

Miles smiles. Photo © 2015 Charles Giuliano.

Miles licks his chops. Photo © 2015 Charles Giuliano.

Ornette

Free Jazz
Ornette Coleman
Changed everything
Miles beyond Davis
Way out there
Now mainstream
Where it all went
For younger players
True genius
Tipping point
Post Bop
Lunch
Probing a polymath
Unstructured dialogue
Following his lead
Thread of thoughts
Told of stomach probe
Asked the doctor
For a look down the tube
To see his innards
Endless curiosity
Enduring visionary
Recalling outrageous
Performances
Crashing over me
Waves of textured sound
Beyond comprehension
Submitting to
Rushes of engagement
Against interpretation
Not making sense

Catching the new wave

When one and one

Make three

Lunch with Ornette Coleman. Photo © 2015 Charles Giuliano.

Philip Glass

Lunch with
Philip Glass
Eons ago
Preview for
Concert at Sanders Theatre
Across the table
Snapping away
Shooting tungsten 160
Soft moody color
Pushed E-6 process
Developed in my bathroom
Charles he said
Becoming annoyed
As I switched Pentaxes to
Black and white
I can't talk to your camera
Listened taking notes
Conversation now
Long forgotten
Pictures
Capturing that
Expressive face
Intense but
Brief encounter
Lasting forever

A pensive Philip Glass. Photo © 2015 Charles Giuliano.

BB King

The left hand
Fluttering like a butterfly
Picking a stinging line
That unique
Widely-imitated
Vibrato
Coaxed from the
Full-bodied Gibson
He called
Lucille
The original one
Rescued from a fire
Was stolen
There would be
Other Lucilles
Two wives
Fifteen children
Countless musicians
Clapton to Hendrix
Called him their father
Up from the Delta
Mississippi sharecropper
Beale Street in Memphis
From there to
Stages of the world
Portly
Indeed larger than life
Cast a long shadow
Now faded to
Black and blues

Blues man B.B. King influenced rock guitarists.
Photo © 2015 Charles Giuliano.

John Cage

Sweet and charming
Avant-garde master
Sly prankster
John Cage
Made edible paper
Rugg Road in Allston
List of natural ingredients
Selected by
Tossing coins
Chance operations
Evoking ancient oracle
I Ching
Inspired he told me
Seeing homeless boys
In Brazil
Boiling paper
To fill their stomachs
Video shown
Each semester
First meeting of
Avant-garde seminar
Boston University
Included his score
For rests
Performed by David Tudor
Stop watch and piano
4' 33"
We sat quietly
Hearing ambient sound
In the room
Mind wandering

Filling a brief
Interval of time
For the students
Nothing happened
Discussion that followed
Total outrage
What is art
The more they ranted
The better I liked it
Established a dialogue
In meetings that followed
Ever more outrageous
They came to understand
Learning to listen
Great art can be
About nothing
Which is to say
Everything including
The sound of silence

John Cage with edible papers.
Photo © 2015 Charles Giuliano.

Bethel

Back roads
1947 Pontiac
Big and comfy
Traffic got intense
Destination
Bethel, New York
AKA Woodstock
Max Yasgur's farm
Through Hasidim villages
Stores with shelves stripped clean
Parked and hiked
With Amber and Joey
Long country road
Top of the hill
Swarms far as eye could see
Mudslides
Three days of peace and music
MC Wavy Gravy
Birth and drug reports
Filling time
Between sets
Made it backstage
Press credentials
Copters flying in
Musicians and food
Grapes and champagne
Hanging out
Used the port-a-potty
Not rank
Like the ones for the kids
Perk and privilege

Waited my turn
Out popped
Ravi Shankar
Hands clasped
Mutual bow
Hard act to follow

American Pie

Eastern Shuttle
Flight home from New York
Sunday concert
Symphony Hall
Bad weather
On Logan runway
Taxied past
Crashed plane
Don McLean
Height of fame
Later media invited
Hotel suite
Sprawled on a couch
Ungainly disheveled
Squinting nearsighted
Live TV crew setup
Where are the usual snacks
Don Delacey laid back
PR guy ordered a six pack
That's enough for Metrano
How 'bout the rest of us
Someone asked the obvious
What about American Pie
Don't want to talk about it
Then why are we here
Bolting up
Looking at me intently
Finger pointing
The minute you walked in the room
I knew you were an asshole
Duly noted in the press

What a jerk
One trick pony
Sic transit
Gloria mundi

Tulips

Dressing room
Playboy Club
Boston
Long gone
Bunnies with cotton tails
Shooting pool
With ersatz whales
Look but don't touch
No dating
Absurd falsetto
Strumming ukulele
Tiptoe Through the Tulips
Deranged campy fun
My date snickering
Brink of cracking up
Miss Vicki
Married her on the Tonight Show
Pained askance glances
Opportunist's expression
Talking about sources
Vintage vaudeville tunes
Enthusiasm for old 78s
Oh Mr. Giuliano he gushed
Over-the-top enthusiasm
I just love those records
Push the labels
Up to my face
Smell them
Deep lingering inhale
Look of euphoria
Shelia lost it

Doubled over laughing
Sunday Herald feature
Aunt Catherine
Huge fan
Every family dinner
Tell me about
Tiny Tim
Pushing up
Daisies

King Mycerinus Enthroned. Photo collage © 2015 Charles Giuliano.

Coptic Pot

Restoring all those stone vessels
Looking for new challenge
Exploring all the shelves
Found fragments
Large, brightly painted vessel
Tall and cylindrical
Bottom missing
Pieced it together
Stunning design patterns
From Coptic Christian era
Evened the base
Balanced imposing
Free standing
When finished
Up the stairs to the office
Busting with pride
Displayed my latest creation
Curators freaked out
Where did you get that
Put it back
Even now
Never seen the light
Of day

Agitprop

After college
Tried to get hired as
A welder
My uncle Freddie said
If you want to be an artist
Get a trade
It didn't work
Flunked the test
Not like making sculptures
Got depressed
Went to the museum
Often visited
During high school
A few blocks away
Had to face Dad
That night
When will you get a job
Hated living at home
Bright idea
I'll apply here
Director's office
Perry T. Rathbone
May I help you
His secretary said
Looking for a job
Janitors and guards
Apply in the basement
Actually thought of
Something curatorial
That just isn't done
Do you mind if I ask

Wasting your time
Would you object
Well if you insist
Quick decision
What department
Egypt seemed interesting
May I help you
Yes looking for a job
Get out I'll call security
May I speak to a curator
We get nuts like you
Becoming agitated
All the time
What's the problem Mary
William Stevenson Smith
Asked from his office
This young man wants a job
How interesting
Come in
Sit down
Shifting papers to make room
What did you have in mind
I'll do anything
Called in assistant curator
Edward L.B. Terrace
Well Bill
There's the basement
Worked there
Two and a half years
Never got to be
A welder

Dust Bowl

First day of work
Egyptian Department
Sat in the office
Instructed to read
Become familiar
Staff took turns
Taking me to lunch
Tours of the collection
Old Kingdom
Dynasty Four and Five
Giza pyramids
King Mycerinus
Excavated for Boston
George Andrew Reisner
Crafty horse trader
Swapped Ankhhaf
For arduous excavation
Furniture turned to dust
Removed layer by layer
Tomb of Hetep Heres
Mother of Pharaoh
Royal tombs all went
To Cairo
Like Tutankhamun's
The cursed Howard Carter
Cushy job it seemed
Listen and learn
Couple of weeks later
Dr. Smith said
Come with me
Gate to the basement

Huge roll of keys
Opened vast wing
Rows of shelves
Walls of vitrines
Piles of crates
Abandoned for decades
You'll work here
Turn straw into gold
Started with sweeping
Eight barrels of dirt
Coal miner
Black lung disease
Before lunch
Washed up
Put on suit
MFA's
Youngest curator
Before there were interns

Hearts

Behind huge rack
Enormous stone fragments
My antique desk
Under narrow window
Headless seated sculpture
Obscure early Pharaoh
Primitive inscription
Facing me
Discovered piled up
Mummies
Organs in canopic jars
Outer layers
Painted plaster
Crossed wings
Sacred incantations
Heart scarabs missing
Shucked like oysters
Harvested by thieves
Wrist bracelets looted
Eternal peace violated
My neighbors
Fellow cave dwellers
Dead silent companions
Ancient restive spirits
Making peace with
Their disturbed Ka
Made paper hearts
Healing the wounds
Restored harmony
Servant of the afterlife
From museum's library

Borrowed vintage copy of
I Ching
Consulted the oracle
Transcribed daily in a journal
With thoughts and poems
Internship of
Work and meditation
Internal journey
Wanderjahr
As staycation

Eternal Rest. Photo collage © 2015 Charles Giuliano.

Shards

Basement swept
Mopped
Asked for white paint
Buckets delivered
The entire basement
Spotless
Shelves cleared and washed
Objects dusted
Plastic sheets cut and taped
Preventing further dirt
Massive project
Took months
Given Neal as assistant
Reported tasks completed
Dr. Smith inspected
On to next project
Soaking salt from limestone blocks
Flaking off fragile surfaces
Walls of a mastaba
One small tank
Taking years
Suggested plastic wading pool
Inside beams set on sponges
Stone slabs placed on them
Pump to flush weekly
Hose to nearby sink
Accelerated the job
Mastabas rebuilt
Trained to fix stone vessels
Bill Young's conservation lab
Opened old crates

Shards from Giza
And the more ancient Zawiet El Aryan
Early Dynastic site
Sorted on rows of folding tables
All over the basement
Daunting puzzle
Matched by color and shape
Taped when clicked
Possibilities exhausted
Clay fitted to contour
Shifted to missing areas
Filled with plaster
Sanded to shape
Meticulous craft
Structurally sound
Pots restored
About a hundred
Trompe l'oeil painting
Plate of Ka Ba
Early pharaoh
His cartouche
Only known inscription
After Narmer
Ruler of Upper and Lower Egypt
On display
At the MFA
Those rocks inspired
My book
Shards of a Life

WILD

Alone all day
Vast Egyptian basement
Morning coffee
Fresh hot rolls from the kitchen
Lunch breaks
Coming up for air
Exploring galleries
Alone or lonely
Brought in my painting
Bright yellow textured monochrome
Livened up the ancient gloom
Like my friend Jim
In the classical department
Could have had anything from
Museum's storage
For the office
Preferred my own work
Much more cheerful
Asked to remove it
By Edward L. B. Terrace
Uptight curator
Later murdered in Egypt
Brought in a radio
Piercing the funereal silence
Dialed to WILD
Soul station from nearby Roxbury
Music to soothe long days
Months and years
A guard dropped in to say
Mr. Rathbone
Passing by with visitors

Asked if you can
Turn down the radio
Or change the station
To classical music
How old school and
Droll

Shango

The Classical and Egyptian departments
Separated by a door
Left open by tradition
Under quirky and witty curator
Cornelius Vermeule
A charming and delightful eccentric
Over there
They were always laughing
Having fun
Compared to the Gypos
As he called us
So serious and silent
Jim Jacobs popped up one day
Student of Emily's at BU
In elegant suits and
Shoes from Brooks Brothers
Suggested we have lunch
Stuck in traffic on Comm Ave
On the way to Locke Ober's
In the convertible
He singing along poorly
Up on the Boardwalk
Me getting ever more nervous
Watching the time
Demanded we turn back
Grabbed a sub sandwich
Rushed to the basement
That was a bust
Tried again
After work and off the clock
Apartment shared with Phil Bleeth

Friends for life
He lives in Thailand
I the dignified Egyptologist
Watched in horror
As they got into a food fight
Decades later Shango
Came to my book launch
At the Mount
His conversation with
Mark St. Germain
Inspired this suite
Of basement tapes

MFA classical curator Cornelius Vermeule had a great sense of humor.
Photo © 2014 Charles Giuliano.

Diocletian

Jim had curious duties
In the classical department
No heavy lifting
Studying the coins
Walking Cornelius'
Dalmatian named for
Emperor Diocletian
When he and Emily were away
Feeding the dog and
Birds Casper and Polux
Now and then joined him on rounds
Changing the salts in vitrines
Baked in a kiln
From red back to blue
Restored to the cases
Absorbing moisture
Opposite the office
A vitrine with odd objects
Clay figure with outstretched arms
Across them a broken arm
Know what that means
It was the era of the Beatles
I Want to Hold Your Hand
We laughed at the in joke
One day
Hunkered over the Greek pots
Examining a red figure kylix
Naked men humping
Cornelius came up behind me
Do you read Greek Charles
He translated the inscription

Hold still

Looking about the gallery

Told me how to find the

Dirty pots

You can see the grease stains

Sweaty foreheads pressed to the glass

During museums tours

Shared that information

It made the class

Much more fun

Them wild and crazy

Greeks

Knew how to party

Jim Jacobs on the terrace of The Mount. Photo © 2015 Charles Giuliano.

Jim Jacobs with his airplane. Photo © 2015 Charles Giuliano.

Ankhhaf

First true portrait
Polychromed bust
Vizier Anhkhaf
Before Sesostris III, Nefertiti, or Ankhenaten
Compelling naturalism
Nose broken
Lidded eyes
Weary midlife face
Found at Giza
Studio of chief sculptor
May have been prototype
For next Pharaoh
Died before his father
Greatest single treasure
MFA's Ancient Egyptian Art
During WWII
Too priceless to risk losing
Possible bombing
Replaced by plaster cast
Precise replica
Original with other treasures
Safe at the Clark
In Williamstown
Replica in my
Basement domain
Project to restore the nose
Took the initiative
Clay and plaster
Then painted
Perfect fit
Proudly displayed

To Dr. Smith
He freaked
To me
He looked whole
As he was
Thousands of years ago
The Prince
Would understand
Smiling from
Serene afterlife

Omnibus

Twilight in Arizona. Photo © 2015 Charles Giuliano.

Every Other Sunday

Maid's day off
Poring over Sunday Herald
Debating what to see
Spread out
Living room
1760 Beacon Street
Heart of Brookline
Office on the first floor
Dinner at 5:30 p.m
My job to
Turn on lights in waiting room
Open door for patients
At 7 p.m.
Monday, Wednesday, Friday
Mom's hours
Tuesday and Thursday Dad's
Never on Sunday
Dinner and a movie
Downtown
Theatres along Washington Street
Between department stores
Jordan's, Filene's, Raymond's
Art Deco Paramount
Smaller Mayflower
Huge Metropolitan
Shooting gallery
Live ammo
The Laugh Movies
Distorting mirror in front
Funny to see yourself
Large or small

Like eat me drink me
I begged for cowboys
John Wayne, Randolph Scott
Loved seeing horses
Long afternoons
B movie, previews
Lowell Thomas Movietone News
Eyes and ears of the world
Then the feature
Mom insisted on
Exeter Street Theatre
In the former
Spritualists' Temple
Séances in the basement
Every Alec Guinness picture
Alastair Sim, Margaret Rutherford
Hilarious Terry-Thomas
Foreign films
Then rare and sophisticated
No candy or popcorn
At the Exeter
On Saturday afternoons
Walked to
Coolidge Corner or Cleveland Circle
The Egyptian in Brighton
Exotic lobby
Longer walk
Where I saw thrilling
King Solomon's Mines
Stopped for penny candy
During the trudge home

Matinees

Saw everything

Didn't seem to matter

Miracles in the dark

Took time to realize

They weren't all great

Some better than others

Wondered why

Birth of a critic

Hook

Branding the latest iPhone 6
Nobody really cares
Who did it
Some geek from
Silicon Valley
No doubt well paid
Money not fame
Identity irrelevant
Functionality counts
Developing technology
Slow and tedious process
Like creating
Abstract art
I explained to a friend
Most people
Glaze over trying
To comprehend the arcane
Humanize it
Put a face
On the concept
Like the telephone
Alexander Graham Bell
After years of effort
Simply said
Mr. Watson come here
I need you
That all important
Anecdote
Eureka moment
We relate to that
Nobody gives a fig

About the science
How can your
Work engage us
Pitch the
Sizzle not the steak
Then as you say
The image speaks for
Itself but
How to get us
To look
Bait the hook with
Something tasty
To chew on

Son of a Beach

A summer day
At the beach
Ocean breezes
The Hamptons
Or anywhere upscale
Where posh women lunch
Slather with sunblock
Bake by the sea
Afternoons before
Cocktails at the club
Where husbands golf
Cutting deals on the greens
Idle conversation
Gossip of affairs
Latest rumors then
Their children
Inevitable one-upmanship
My son admitted to Harvard
Proclaimed triumphantly
Legacy connection
Several generations
Old money
Another chimed in Yale
Son of Skull and Bones
Yet again Williams
Trumping everyone
My kid got into RISD
Not doctor, lawyer or MBA
My son the artist
Sure path to
Fame and fortune

Old Mr. Boston

Northeast Harbor, Maine
Summer cottages
Mansions actually
Views of the ocean
Fourth of July
Visiting a friend
Party on the rocks
Enormous home behind
Cheese Whiz on Ritz crackers
Boiled hot dogs and buns
All American it seems
Going all out on the booze
Old Mr. Boston Gin
Cott's not Schwepp's for tonic
Scotch you never heard of
Instant headache
Generic beer
Yankee celebration
Old money
Never spent
Socked into trust funds
Honored
Just to be there
Feeling oddly
Outclassed
By tightwads

Hippy

A true story
No lie
Used to mean
Dropping acid
Smoking dope
Being groovy
Sweet bird of youth
This morning
Old man
Waiting for cortisone shot
Bum knee
Email message
Colleague's update
Hip surgery scheduled
Second one a week later
Postponed
Surgeon tore his rotator cuff
Good grief
Decades after Woodstock
New definition for a
Hippy

Duck

Duck last night
Weekly Chinese Mondays
Sushi House
North Adams
Fun with friends
Tried new dishes
Irving had
Seafood hot pot
David and Astrid
Variations of fish
Joy the hostess
Asked how I liked it
Had long considered
On the menu
Not quite Chinatown
Good for the Berkshires
Told her about
Peking Duck in
Shanghai
Just incredible
Elegant restaurant
Complex preparation
Made me think of
Jane
Fellow Scorpio
Age separated by days
Always celebrated
With a duck
She cooked for us
Such a treat
My favorite

Y Not

Bought a nice chicken
At Big Y
Buck a pound
Sticker two dollars off
Paid three
Sunday dinner
In the oven at four
Slow roasted
Herbs de Provence
Basted with
Sauvignon Blanc
House wine from
Trader Joe
Cases each summer
Fresh and cheap
Rested the bird
Astrid the skilled
Saucier chef
Hens of the woods mushrooms
The reduced wine drippings
Carved half
Couple of nights later
The other side
Heated in the gravy
Rice and al dente broccoli
Carcass tomorrow's meal
Soup with stem of the mushrooms
Carrots and celery
Boiled nicely
Three and perhaps four meals
For the two of us

Living well
Dollar a day
Beating the odds
Having fun
Robert said
Daily dialogue
Arts and culture
Consigliore
Boulevardier and aesthete
My friend
Bucket list
You and I must dine
Three star Michelin restaurant
What would that cost
I asked
He has done it round the world
Other people's money
CBS expense account
Back in the day
Meals to die for
Exquisite service.
Trust me
It's worth it
Have to splurge now and then
Ok but
More then than now

Movietone News

Memories of WWII
The Greatest Generation
Uncles in the war
All survived
Heroes and not
Kept a scrapbook
Cut and pasted
From Life Magazine
Later made model airplanes
Mary McKnight
Our scary maid
Help was hard to find
Squeezing a bag of white lard
Dot of yellow dye
Ersatz butter
Proto margarine
Ration book at the butcher
Nat's in Allston
Always a slice of
Baloney for the kid
Sugar rare
Lots of Spam
OK on gas
Doctors were essential
Sunday cartoons
Terry and the Pirates
Racist comic books
Weekly cinema
War footage
Movietone News
Eyes and ears of the world

Voice of Lowell Thomas
Bombed-out Berlin
Image of baby carriage
Indelible
Like Eisenstein's Potemkin
In the alley
Enormous woodpile
Ersatz fort
Played cowboys and Indians
Japs and Germans
Everyone wanted
To be GI Joe
In Hamburg
Bombs fell
Near hospital where
Astrid was born
Her youthful memories
More horrific
Than mine

Reasonable

With platitudes
We greet each other
Lacking sincerity
Lives measured
Spoons of sugar
In cups of tea
How are you
Nobody wants to know
Not really
About our aches and pains
Thoughts on the cosmos
Reasonable I say
To the waiter and clerk
Cocktail conversations
Waiting for their reaction
The unexpected
Occasional laugh
Reasonable
What's that
At times
Meaning
Not good or bad
Coping best I can
Thanks for asking
Response to which
I hear you
Right-on bro
Have a nice day
Or the more terse
Have a good one
A good what I ask

As if anyone

Gives a damn

Life measured in cups of tea.

Guido's

Upscale Berkshire market
Opposite the former Dakota
Now gone fusion
Dakoto
Just up the road from
Mazzeo's
Restaurant renowned for meats
Specialty sold at
Guido's
Where we pack the freezer
With their awesome sausage
Summers on the grill
Everything pricey
High quality
After an appointment
In Pittsfield
Astrid shopped
Admired two tomatoes
One yellow
The other deep greenish red
Not yet ripe
Too firm to the touch
Heirlooms she explained
The red one cost
Five bucks
Didn't know it weighed a pound
Couple of weeks to
Memorial Day
Let's plant them
Each year iffy
Come harvest time

But lots cheaper

Guido's smoked pork chop with sauerkraut, Guinness, and tarragon.

Lobster Thermidor

Exquisite Sunday dinners
Beacon Street Brookline
Novak's
Elegant restaurant
Walking distance
From home
Dad was such a sport
Ordering our favorite
Lobster Thermidor
The meat removed
Sherry, cream, cheese, mushrooms
Baked in its shell
Served on a fresh napkin
Struck me as
Decadent extravagance
Savoring every bite
Most delicious treat
Followed by
Baked Alaska
How amazing
In a clay pot
Inducing Lisa
Not to cancel
Annual Kentucky Derby Party
Breast cancer benefit
Problem with venue
Have it in our gallery
Short notice
She reluctant
I'll bring lobster thermidor
Blurted out in jest

Yesterday in the gallery
Everyone ragged on me
Where's the lobster mate
Great party
Ladies in hats
Too many mint juleps
My horse won
American Pharaoh
Sorry guys
My bad
Maybe next year

Race to the Finish. Photo © 2015 Charles Giuliano.

God is Dead

Nothing new actually
Shocking once
Not any more
Be reasonable
Seven days
Not bloody likely
More like billions
Before that
Vast emptiness
Soup that exploded
Big bang
Eventually us
Not by some God
Created in our image
Fear and superstition
Filling the void
Huge cover-up
The Bigger Lie
Many versions
All wrong
Providing order
Repression through
True believers
Total bonkers
Utter nonsense
No heaven and hell
Just here and now
Rationality
Doing the right thing
Basic humanism
Moral existentialism

Divinity as logic
And ethics
Not preached
By priests

A lunar eclipse evokes the vast unknown. Photo © 2015 Charles Giuliano.

Lights Out

Ever expanding universe
Outer limits
Unfathomable
Distances
Measured in light years
Yet an end in sight
Our beyond
When stars flicker out
The eventual dark sky
No more energy
Not defined by our God
Seemingly so focused on us
Inhabiting a tiny planet
Tail end of
Nowhere
Where dinosaurs roamed
Like them
Facing extinction
A matter of time
Racing toward that
Inevitable endgame
Through our greed and abuse
Squandered resources
Not on my watch
Generations from now
Beyond prayer and redemption
Triage and regeneration
No resurrection or ascension
Heaven and hell
Moot points
Figments of human-centric

Mumbo gumbo
Where will God be
Or care
When all of this is
Entropy
To dust
Littered space
Aftermath of creation

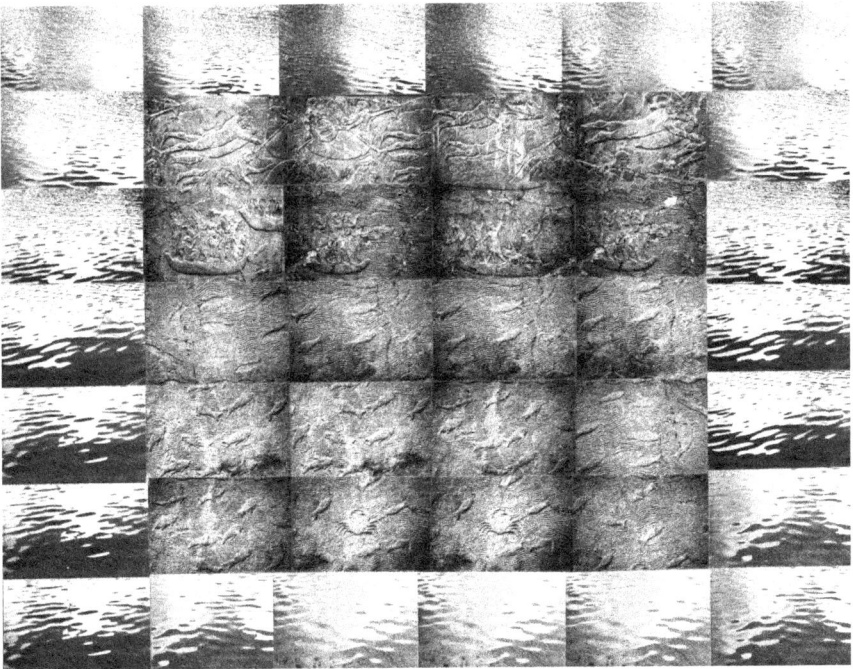

Time and Tide. Photo collage © 2015 Charles Giuliano.

Kiss Me Kate

Kensington Palace says
Catherine, Duchess of Cambridge
Kate Middleton
To you and me
Born a commoner
More or less
Before the frenzy
Gave birth to a girl
Not of itself remarkable
Here's the hitch
Fourth in line
For the top job
Monarch of the realm
Once the imperial
Keeper of Welsh Corgis
Is but a memory
Greatest accomplishment
Defined at birth
Nothing else matters
A life of trivia
Present for ceremonies
Signifiers of
All things British
Like fish and chips
Served hot
Wrapped in greasy
Media

Bang Bang

Every boy
Needs a gun
To shoot other kids
Like the Wild West
Bang Bang
Cowboys and Indians
Good guys and bad guys
Cops and robbers
Christmas
FAO Schwarz
With Mom's friend
Alice Moran
Tried on Tom Mix
Nah not that one
Insisted on
Hopalong Cassidy
Two guns
Double six-shooters
Quick draw
Twice the money
Got my wish
Guns in America
Not toys anymore
Kids today
Play with real ones

Apathy

Vividly recalling protest years
Young Americans
Marches and riots
Anti-war
Gays and women
Stonewall
Civil Rights
Selma
Malcolm X
Told them
We tried to change the world
Believed in things
Chastising their apathy
Hoping to inspire
From back of the class
Student responded
Plaintive voice
Oh Mr. Giuliano
You're so
Joan Baez

Fear Eats Itself

Savagery of family
Bonfire of creativity
Feeding the flames
Scavenged memory
Wild beast
Untamed psyche
Trapped
Gnawing at its leg
Ferocious amputation
Four reduced to three
Limping away
Wounded
But free

Making Art

You can make art
In whatever form
Or have friends
Perhaps not both
Which is why
Some of the best ones
Drink, die young
Have shattered lives
It takes that much
Digging up the stuff
Buried inside
Battered and formed
Traumas of experience
Cannibalizing relationships
Ripping into family
Working on the energy
Oblivious to feelings
Brushing off other opinions
Mad bull
Forging ahead
Monsters and minotaurs
Perhaps celebrated
Emotionally skeletal
By the end
Eaten inside
Consuming cancer of creation
Or not
Making some art
Modest success
Not total gonzo
Small triumphs here and there

Life well lived
Cautious hedonism
Nestled in academia
With tenure
That early demise
End of risk taking
Modestly pushing the
Envelope
The life more protected
Not fully explored
The art game
Has so few
Big winners
When probed
Too often
Biggest losers
Celebrated by
Vicarious vulgarians
Reviled in biographies
Those that knew
Or even loved them
Who respected
No boundaries

Beauty of the Beast

Labyrinth of self
How not to get lost
Into the maze
Hall of mirrors
False impressions
Faceted cubism
Confronting
The Minotaur
Bull and human
Beast of art
Devouring sacrifices
Boys and maidens
Untested warriors
Withering
Overpowering
Inner demons
Matador
Picador's taunting insults
Enraging the monster
Deadly charge
Sharp horns
No ole
Empty arena
Studio devoid of spectators
Lacking a cape
Bare sword
Brutal combat
Powerful and triumphant
Unwinding the string
Of memory
Exiting the cave

Retracing steps
Brandishing severed head
Signifier
Of creativity

Battle with Centaurs in the Forrest. Photo collage © 2015 Charles Giuliano.

Sisyphus Now

Not like Camus
The boulder
Up and down
The Hill
Existential Labor
Far too monumental
More mundane
Loading and unloading
The dishwasher
Tasks of the everyday
Lives measured
Laundry washed and folded
The grinding reality
Actual lives
Utterly devoid
Of metaphors
Drudgery of surviving
Getting by
Little pleasures
The occasional better meal
A few pints at the pub
Something on TV
Rutting to make children
Devoid of
Highfaluting
Grandiosity
Triumph of the ordinary
Servant in the court of
Pharaoh
Not buried
With exotic treasures

No Canopic jars
For the heroic
Everyman

Egyptian Book of the Dead. Photo collage © 2015 Charles Giuliano.

Big Easy

Every day
Is Mardi Gras
Bourbon Street
Starts at noon
Gets more intense
Hustlers and panhandlers
Getting an early start
Rubes in beads
From the burbs
Looking for adventure
Lunch at Acme Oyster
Favorite destination
No lines
Grilled oysters
Gumbo
Side of jambalaya
Moving on
Getting more intense
Didn't tip ugly queen
For a picture
Hey honey I do this for a living
Out of the madness
To Jackson Square
Riff band blasting
More loud than good
Vamping for tips
Café du Monde
Of Course
Grabbed our seats
Tourists waited
Taking a load off

Moved to the river

Nation splitter

Ending here

Dog-tired

Slogging home

Tomorrow is

Another day

Had enough of Bourbon St.

Till next time

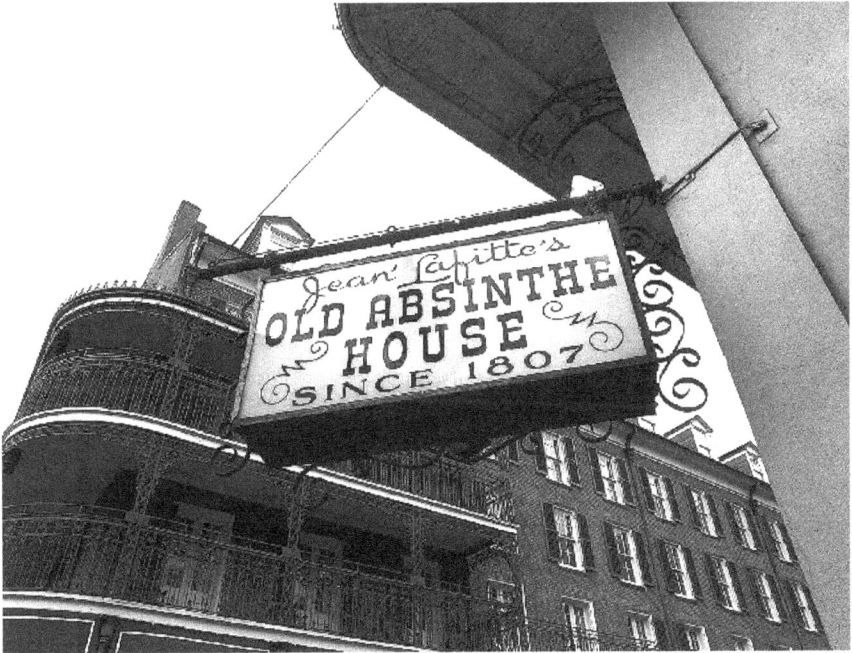

Bourbon Street in the French Quarter. Photo © 2015 Charles Giuliano.

Tennessee Williams' Hotel Plays

Rainy day
The French Quarter
Hermann-Grima House
Seedy Southern mansion
Crowded into run down rooms
Glimpses of past glory
Days of elegance
Long gone by
Audience jammed in
Inches from actors
Fantasy fragments
Fevered detritus
Fueled by rum
Cigarettes burning
Lamp of squalid imagination
Setting more than sets
Ambiance as art
Snippets of characters
Sketches from compulsive
Work for the sake of it
Not making sense or
Meant to
Drinking the Kool Aide
Degenerate characters
Last gasps
Compelling glimpses
Les Tableaux Vivant
Times indeed
So Picayune
Scent of decayed
Magnolias

Tennessee Williams' Hotel Plays. Photos courtesy of Ride Hamilton, copyright 2015.

Ms. Divine

On the road
Kindah Thelma and Louise
Actually Lynda and The Divine
Hit Bourbon Street
Girls gone wild
Booze to excess
Quest for sex
The Divine
Game for more
Commissioned a private dance
Squalid back room
Dimly lit
On a small table
David on a pedestal
For more coin
Giggle and grope
Sleazy bloke
Gyrating about
Working his junk
Until with a thud
Slipped and fell
Crashing her fantasy
Rude awakening
Look but don't touch
Big easy does it

Killing Time

Dismal period in my life
Future in the balance
Stoned with friends
In Cambridge
Killer weed
Clear cold winter night
Walking home to Brookline
Not liking
Being there after graduation
Dealing with mistakes
On the Harvard bridge
Looking up at the bright moon
Silvered clouds
Moving slowly against black sky
Feeling the force of nature
Turmoil of fevered thought
Looking down at the icy Charles
To be or not to be
Took my watch off
Dropped in the river
Of no regrets
Freezing the moment
Tortured sublime
Of prodigal
Youth

On the Beach

International weekends
Former Herald librarian
Offered us standby
Weekly flights
Just seventy-five bucks
Good to go
Told the boss
Friday afternoon
OK but come back
With your Sunday piece
Small plane
Refueled Newfoundland
Then Reykjavik
Staggered into hall
Steak with Béarnaise sauce
Suburban hotel
Bus into town
Havarti cheese
Open faced sandwiches
Swan Lake
Royal Danish Ballet
Next night
Live sex show
Cost extra
Didn't want to pay
Concierge disappointed
Took pity for being alone
Got me comps
Another ballet
On the Beach
Nuclear survivors

Dancers nude
Free sex show
Breakfast conversation
How was the evening
Downtown storefront
Folding chairs
A platform
They fucked
We watched
Had some wine
Seems I got
The better deal

Markland, Nova Scotia. Photo collage © 2015 Charles Giuliano.

Bistro

The Marais
Rafael's funky loft
Not yet chic
Rue de la Roquette
Near Place du Bastille
Spring break
Spartan studio
Cold at night
Louvre by day
Shooting slides
Stopping for snacks
On the way home
The fromagerie
Hundreds of cheeses
Un piece de chèvre s'il vous plaît
Quesque chèvre
Il demand
Les touts sont chèvre
La pointing embarrassed
With bread and wine
Then off for dinner
Up and down the street
Looking here and there
The perfect bistro
Like in old movies
Lace curtains
She confronted me
Reservation
Not really
Showed me the book
Months in advance

Threw a fit

Je suis un fameux American

Je demand a manger maintenant

Tout de suite

Call the cops if you like

I'm not moving

Until I'm fed

Young and handsome

Arrogant and a bit mad

She checked me out

Top to bottom

In that manner of French women

The staff giggled

Reassured me

It will be just a minute

The owner's table

With her lover

Impressed

You put on quite a show

Intimidated her

How exciting

Bravo

Advised on the traditional menu

Then after coffee and brandy

Let me show you Paris

Till dawn

Staggered embrace

Under a street lamp

Bon matin mon frere

Nous sommes des amis

Pour tout la vie

Luck of the Non-Irish

The nuns loved
St. Patrick's Day
Helped us to cut out
Green shamrocks
Decorating our dining room
Having wonderful fun till
Kathleen from Cork
Maid of the Kelleher clan
Sisters one after the other
Parading through our home
Like ersatz Ellis Island
Made fresh soda bread
Bitter laments
American butter is not like Irish butter
Scoffed at my enthusiasm
Now what right have you
The nerve and gall
Yer muther may be a wee bit
But yer not a'tall
Heavens no
Yer not Irish
Yer Eay-Tal-Eians
So don't ye go shamrockin
Saints preserve us
Erin go Brach yerself

To Ur is Inhuman

Mesopotamia
Land of milk and honey
Garden of Eden
Mother of us all
Tigris and Euphrates
Ruins of Ur
Gilgamesh
Ziggurats reaching to God
People of the Book
Tribes of Abraham
Golden Calf
Graven Images
Iconoclasm
Modern Iraq
Custodians of civilization
Ancient monuments
Humanist heritage
Smashed by ISIS
Millennial artifacts
Reduced to rubble
Cultural barbarism
Beheading Infidels
Evoking Allah
Destroying legacies
Sharia run rampant
Global terrorism
Compelling arguments
For Western
Museums

Jihad

Off with their heads
French Revolution
Reign of Terror
Daily event
Mobs
Sans Culottes
Bringing lunch and wine
Madame Thérèse Defarge
Front row
Save me a seat
One by one
From King and Queen
Aristocrats to servants
Eventually the Directory
Danton then Robespierre
Petered out
Got boring
Crowds dwindled
Other things to do
Some escaped
Jacques Louis David
Tale of Two Cities
Now ISIS
On video
Bathed in blood
Harvesting organs for sale
Motivating recruits
Ranks swelling
Inexplicable apathy
From Arab world
Relative inaction

Moderate Islam
Guardedly cautious
Minced words from Obama
Terrorists
Not Islamic Extremists
What then to call
Jihad
Return to barbarism
Evoking Allah

Adams

Nothing ever happens
In Adams
Our perfect Berkshire home
View of Mt. Greylock
From the deck
Monday night Chinese
Weekly meeting at
Sushi House
Where Joy serves
Tasty varied food and margaritas
To starving artists
Catching up on stuff
Busy summer season
Eric recounting his annual
Beach Party on Eagle Street
Free gifts for kids
Plastic pails and shovels
Lots of hot dogs
Everyone enjoying event
Later misadventure
Handicapped man
Stuck in museum's elevator
During opening after
The party
Took three hours to
Get him out
Then it got dark
Did you hear about the terrorist
Living in Adams
Gail and Phil said
From across the table

She grew up there
Alexander Ciccolo, 23
Son of Boston Police captain
Intent on mayhem
Plotting massacre
For Isis
Not in our little village
The madman next door
Kept to himself
Neighbors said
Bought pressure cooker
At local Walmart
Stash of weapons
Molotov cocktails
With evil intent
Heartless in the heartland
No more
Thornton Wilder
What the fuck happened
To our town

Noblesse

Tenth Earl of Tarrington
Nursed his scotch
Musing languidly
Gazing with no particular focus
From the great house
Into manicured gardens
Behind which woods for hunting
Stretching beyond
Inviting strolling
Dressed snugly in tweed
Shotgun and hound
Occasionally bagging
Fowl for feasting
Or blasting a round
Up the ass of a brash poacher
Intruders on the ancient property
Passed down father to
Eldest son
Since Hastings and all that
Back from the dragoons
Scars to prove
Curious ennui since
Nothing much to do
Season in London
Sessions of Parliament
Balls with debutantes
Evenings at the club
Chums from Oxford
Punters and scullers
Occasional slumming
For the sport of it

Deep sigh
Finished the drink
Toasting the Queen
Walked out to the terrace
Blew his brains
Nothing else to do
Quite

Versailles. Photo collage © 2015 Charles Giuliano.

Jingle Bells

The nun rehearsed us
Little kids
Mt. Alvernia Academy
Christmas pageant
On stage
Singing Jingle Bells
On our wrists
Elastic bands with bells
Told to shake them
Merry tinkling sound
What fun
Leaving
Making way for another class
Woman
Probably a mother
Demanded I give her
My precious souvenir
Sister asked me to collect them
Reluctantly
She insisted
I handed it over
Looked around
Just me
The only one
Heartbroken
Never again
Trusted grown ups

Tats

Cumberland Farms
For milk
Cashier
Customer says
Looking at her hand
New Tat
She twenty-something
Plain features
Yeah
Found it on line
Modified
Wher'd you get it
Williamstown
First
No fourth
He older
Maybe forties
Kindah hitting on her
Got a big one
On my back
Want four more
Me twenty
When I get the money
Something
What the heck
Looking forward to
No brainer
Then what
Angels
In America
Icarus

Daily Scam

Mr. Giuliano
Name mangled
What do you want
Do you need a wheelchair
Not exactly
Free TV
What's the hitch
Solar panels
Maybe
Consolidate credit cards
I'm busy
Thick accent
India or Bangladesh
Like dial-up days
Offshore tech support
Third world boiler rooms
How 'bout those Red Sox man
Or Yankees
Depending on the
Area code
Global scuffle and hustle

Faux

Genuine
Faux pearls
Ersatz authentic
Paranormal
You faux man
No
Faux you
What the faux
Mo faux

Rejuvena

Seniors
Missing out on those
Golden Years
Tired, run down, depressed
Feel young again
Get back in the game
Jog on the beach
Play tennis and golf
Dance the night away
With Rejuvena
See your physician
Ask if it's right for you
Not sold over the counter
Start today
Daily dose
Life-changing experience
Feel like a kid again
Do not take if you have
High blood pressure, diabetes, anemia
May cause headaches, diarrhea, internal bleeding
In rare cases may result in
Strokes, amnesia, blindness, kidney failure, ulcers
Or death

Woody

After midnight
The elderly couple
Drove to the emergency room
Hunched over
Clutching a bulky coat
The receptionist
Asked what ailed him
It's been more than four hours
She looked puzzled
Adjoining bathtubs
Holding hands
Pressing close and whispering
He revealed the problem
With a knowing look
Understood and was
Impressed
Taking a seat
Watching TV
Generic boring program
Typical triage
Waited a couple of hours
Gradually
Icicle melted
Murmuring
They went home
Softly

Valentine's Day

Evening class
BU
Sparsely attended
Next week asked
What gives
Valentine's Day
You can't expect us to come
Not on the school calendar
I noted
Same with Halloween
In their hearts
Not minds it seems
How delusional
Different story
Love
Conquers all
In the real world
Explain that
To the boss

Rubenesque

No more Skinny Minnie
Add curvaceous inches
Have that beautiful bust
You always wanted
No nasty diets
Eat food you crave
Enjoy pizza, pasta and ice cream
Cookies whenever
Dawn to dusk
As the urge strikes
Snack between meals
Live it up
Gluten and carbs to the max
Add gorgeous inches
In just a few weeks
Slip into
Plus-sized lingerie
Throw your weight around
Take up belly dancing
Be the envy of all your friends
And that's not all
Call now and get started
Fun awaits
Operators are standing by
Just pennies per day
Money back guarantee
Just in time
For the Holidays

Beckett Busted

Absurdist
Samuel Beckett
Considered
Deadpan genius
Stone-faced
Buster Keaton
The master
Traveled to USA
Only time
Found him retired
In LA
Last days
Watching television
Godot's waiting room
Star of silent films
Had nothing
To say
Not Endgame
Just mum's
The word
Shot Film
NY July 1964
24 minutes
Beckett's only movie
Checkmate

Charity

Park Street
Cross from the
State House
Homeless woman
Snaggletoothed hag
Ripe as a rotten peach
Hit on me
Hey mister
Howabout
Something to eat
Wouldn't give her
Cash for booze
Called her bluff
Took her to
Dunkin Donuts
Have what you like
Pointed her bony finger
Hungry for
Something freshly baked
Sly impish look
Quick glance toward me
Then ordered
Drink to go with them
I'll have a latte
She said with bravura
Not what I had in mind
Of all the noive
Smile was worth it
Got the best of me
Give unto others
Made her day

The Mount

View from the Terrace
Early June evening
Overlooking formal gardens
The Mount
Berkshire home
Edith Wharton
Elegant setting
Steeped in literature
Ghosts roam the attic
Launch of my book
Shards of a Life
Gathering of friends
Making efforts
To be there
Neighbors from our loft
Members of the International Club
Benno and Jim
Who brought me here
Decades ago
Alice's Breast Flaunt
Poets playwright artists
Ersatz Countess
Astrid and our dream team
Made it all possible
Fine food drink
Dialogue with Susan Wissler
Answering her questions
Interspersed with poems
My first-ever reading
Lots of humor
Well received

Autographing books
My wrist froze up
Getting the word out
Finding readers
Not looking back
Age of Innocence
Lost under her roof
Turning the page
New chapters
To be shared

Susan Wissler director of The Mount. Photo © 2015 Charles Giuliano.

Actor Dennis Hopper was total gonzo during an interview.
Photo © 2015 Charles Giuliano.

Out of the Blue

Mid-afternoon 1980
Copley Plaza Hotel
Dennis Hopper
Low budget movie
Out of the Blue
Starred in and directed
Last minute decision
Asked about pop art collection
Bought with money from
Giant
Worked with James Dean
Twice
Other one
Rebel Without a Cause
Gifted photographer
Coppola gave him cameras
Apocalypse Now
Friends with Andy
Hung at Max's Kansas City
Bought great works
Early and cheap
Lost them all
Hung his head
As if to weep
You had to ask
Worth millions
All gone
Up in smoke
Divorcing gorgeous
Daria Halprin
Star of Antonioni's cult classic

Zabriskie Point
Third of five wives
Excused himself a few times
Doing blow
Ever more whacked
Posed for crazed photo
Followed by Kathy Huffhines
Last appointment
Got the best interview
Shagged him
Can't compete with that
Brilliant career
Ended abruptly
Sitting in a car with boyfriend
Tree fell on them
Freak accident
Moth to flame

Nudie

Elton John invited me to LA
Hanging in Hollywood
Under wing of
Elton's PR guy
Legendary Norm Winter
Wouldn't let me
Open my wallet
Wined and dined
Had expense money
From Herald Traveler
Bash at historic
Saint Francis Hotel
In Frisco
Orgy in the rooms
Norm leaned over
To nude multi-tasking
Lady of leisure
I have a VIP
Can he get in there
Thanks but no thanks
Grabbed tequila
From the open bar
Wandered off
Into the night
Best to forget
Flying back to LA
By way of Burbank
Norm said
Let's visit my friend
Nudie of Hollywood
He was napping

Sized me up
Try this on
Bright orange
Nashville suit of lights
Steaks on grills
Campfires
Up rhinestone legs
Norm flipped
It's you baby
Offer I could not refuse
Made for one-hit wonder
Never picked it up
Just my size
That night
Norm insisted I wear it
To the Troubadour
The Pointer Sisters
Nobody noticed the bling
Different story back in
Beantown
Years later
Peter Wolf asked
Hey Man
Yah still got the suit
Now a museum piece
In plastic wrap
Hanging in the closet
With my
Rock and roll shoes

Charles Giuliano in Nudies of Hollywood sequined suit with Jan Nelson at Castle Hill rock party. Photo © 1972 Steve Nelson.

First Novel

Just before Christmas
Writing feverishly
By hand
Designing cover
Eventually seven pages
Stuck together
First chapter of first novel
Tale of Two Cities
Compelling title
Old West stagecoach
Traveling back and forth
Rawhide the driver
Jake riding shotgun
Fighting off
Bandits and Indians
Tough tobacco-chewing dudes
Sure to be a best seller
When guests arrived
Proudly displaying
My book
Urging each and every one
To read it
Most didn't
With a smile and pat on my head
What a sweet, smart lad
Decades later
Finally launching
First literary effort
This week
At Edith Wharton's
The Mount

Took all this time
To get up
The gumption

Southwest Panorama. Photo collage © 2015 Charles Giuliano.

Wild Party

Moonlight night
Walk to Lighthouse Beach
Past the Hedbloom house
Sloping hill
View of the water
Laughter and music
Sound of scratchy 78
Smoke Gets in Your Eyes
All the kids having fun
Not invited
Getting even
Midweek
When Mom and Dad were
Home in the city
Called everyone I knew
Far away as Marblehead
Sailing buddies
The house was packed
Rock Around the Clock
Tons of beer
Motorcycle gang from Gloucester
Crashed the party
Little sister Pip
Danced with the leader of the pack
Next day she and Lillian
Who we so loved
Surrogate Mom
Cleaned it all up
Kept mum
On the beach that weekend
Peg Usher spilled the beans

She was such a gossip
Mom came home furious
In the bedroom
Closed the door
Read the riot act
List of chores
Or you're not going to
Marblehead Race Week
Worth it
Peter Hedbloom
Later Cambridge neighbor
Looked like a young JFK
Was jealous

Max's

Near Union Square
Mickey Ruskin's
Max's Kansas City
Steak, Lobster, Chick Peas
Summers on the dole
Off-season
Galleries closed
City quiet and empty
The rich in the Hamptons
Happy hour
Nursing sour white wine
Feasting on chicken wings
Dinner many a night
Seventy-five cents
Ringside seat
Floor show
Sweeping in
Brice Barden ersatz Byronesque
With lovely Helen
Later
Candy and Andy
Entourage
Commandeering
Backroom
Under the fluorescent Flavin
Bar tabs
Settled with works
Artist hangout
Weekends
Bridge Tunnel
Banging at the gates

Rarely admitted
Mickey at the door
Ragged and tattered
Looking generic
Waving in regulars
Ropes for dopes
Rene Ricard
Dancing on tables
Before Valerie shot Andy
Factory nearby
Walking home
Full and entertained

Mad Max

Visiting Canadian curator
Business with East Hampton Gallery
My boss Bruno said
Show him the town
Go to Max's
Reluctant tour guide
Asked if he smoked weed
Sure all the time
Bounced into the park
Got a buzz
Toked some
Great ganja
Made our way
Downtown
In a booth
Having a brew
Surrounded by hipsters
Slumped forward
Passed out cold
Avoiding scandal
Taking the blame
Maybe getting banned
Grabbed the sucker
Hauled his ass outside
Propping him up
Knee to the back
Hailed a cab
Got his address
Sent him packing
Next day he fell by
As though nothing happened

Bruno asked
Did he have a good time
Awesome man
What a cool dude
Mush you husky
Or was it
Hush you musky

Pop

Mr. Padziba
Landlord
303 East 11th Street
My storefront
Late 1960s
Called the ancient super
Pop
Apartment opposite me
Hibernated
Rarely sighted
Terrified of
Die Kinder
As he said in a
Craggy accent
Door opened ajar
Catching glimpses
Dust everywhere
Enduring last days
Alone and abandoned
Liles came by
Thanksgiving
We cooked dinner
Junky turkey
Melted butter
Injected under the skin
Moist and tasty
His invention
We made a plate
All the fixings
Asking what do you want
Opened the door

Reluctantly
Same as usual
Surprised smile
Lit up weathered face
Sharing a holiday
Danke

Summer of Love

In my doorway
Lower East Side
She staggered by
Dazed Flower Child
Runaway
Hungry and scared
Dark finger marks
On her neck
Defiled, ashamed
But escaped
No questions asked
Trusting a stranger
Took her in
Shelter and comfort
Walked to Polish deli
Tompkins Square Park
Fed her pirogi at Leshko's
Talked softly calmly
Slept soundly
Next day
Payphone
Begged her to call home
Frantic family
Fearing their anger
Bus ticket
Back to America
Rescue
From a walk
On the wild side

Reverie

Cavernous basement apartment
University Road
The Murder Building
Cambridge
Haunted house
Cheap rent
Round platform
Under windows brimming with plants
Elevated bed
Patterns of Christmas lights above
Walls painted silver and gold
Evocative Shangri-La
Chilling on weed
Distant sirens
Becoming ever louder
Smell of smoke
Must be near
Cool and apathetic
Thunder on the stairs
Pounding at the door
Firemen bursting through
Smoke filled kitchen
Joint in ashtray
Ignited
Janson's History of Art
Tossed in the sink
Doused
Memories of long gone
Reefer madness

Fence

Backyard
East 11th Street
Between buildings
Bags of falling garbage
Tenants too lazy
For curbside trash cans
Rats and alley cats
Remnants of stone terrace
Gangs passing through
Open door
Quick escapes from
Mischief
Asked the landlord
Mr. Padziba
For materials to build
A fence
Delivered load of old doors
Gerry and I put them up
He intrigued
By digging holes in New York
Enclosed and cleaned
Planned garden party
Grill from bed springs and screen
On bricks
Charcoal beneath
Liles flipping burgers
Sangria in a bucket
Faces over the fence
We're the 10th Street gang
And we're hungry
Fed them

Neighbor above

Climbing down fire escape

Greeted nobly

By aristocratic Domingo

In perfect Spanish

Inviting him and his family

Most eloquently

The man froze

Apologized retreating

Outclassed

Fun in the slums

Murder Building

Enormous basement apartment
Heart of Harvard Square
University Road
Alley to Brattle Street
Club Casablanca
Cardell's for eats
Mr. Demmers
Jogged in each day
From Belmont
Son-in-law
Buddy's Sirloin Pit
Up front
Patisserie for
Endless coffee and croissants
Office and living room
Day morphed to night
Cronin's around the corner
Beers just
Four for a buck
Plate of fries
Nights with friends
Next to nada
The Murder Building
Home to rock bands
Chefs and hipsters
The legendary degenerate
Ed Hood the chic Edwina
Building complex
So-called for spectacular crimes
The Boston Strangler
Signature Bow Job

Female victim

Laid out Amazon style

Anthropology student

Harvard professor

Person of interest

Never solved

Alice Cooper party

Trashed my pad

Stuff of legend

Fog of memory

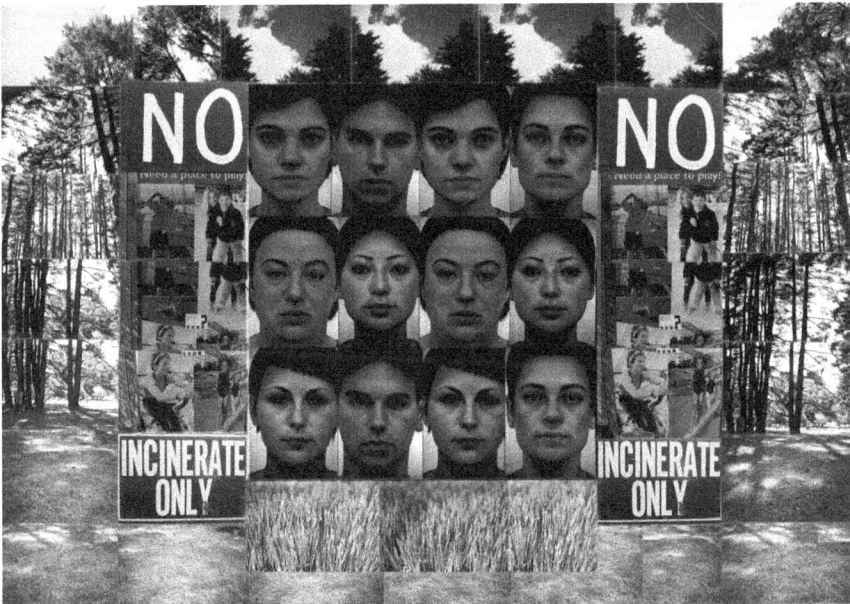

Please Do Not Incinerate. Photo collage © 2015 Charles Giuliano.

.

Birth of Gonzo

Basement apartment
Bill and Sue Cardoso
Globe Magazine editor
After-hours hipster hangout
Telling a lively tale
Softball game
Banging a double
Hard slide
Taking out second baseman
A troubled fellow
Landed on me
Sobbing
It was gonzo man
Total gonzo
Bill perked up
What's that you say Charles
Gonzo
Yeah gonzo
Home run
Over the wall
Outah here
Soon gonzo this and gonzo that
First published Boston Herald
My review of Ten Years After
Szep cartoon in the Globe
Bill talked him into it
Total Gonzo Band
Me on drums
Jimmy Midnight guitar
Blaze signing
Love Potion Number Nine

One gig

Barry got a gonzo vanity plate

Yellow Duster

Soon his short was totaled

Smashed and bashed

Still gonzo

Last of the Mohicans

Journalist Bill Cardoso visiting Charles' Cambridge Apartment.

Easter

Fernando was dating
Susan Sessions
As well as her mother
Cantabridgians
Artists and academics
His father
Distinguished Harvard professor
In my car
Drove to New Hampshire
Her private school
Double date
Me with Chris Capoon
Runaway on the radio
Run run run runaway
Love that tune
Suzie surrogate
Brandeis classmate
My drawing of her
In the yearbook
Lived with Bob Markowitz
Off campus
Later her apartment
Huron Avenue
Many a night hanging out
Acid trip
Painted a mural
Interesting narrow angled space
Her famous hollandaise sauce
Buckwheat noodles
They broke up
Cardoso exchanged glances

Hipster party
Easter Sunday morning
Bill knocking at the door
North End apartment
Insisted that I take him
Formal introduction
They married not long after
Raced to Annisquam
Late for family dinner
My father pissed
Yet again
Taking one
For the team

Giuliano line drawing of Susan Sessions 1963.

Bob Fowler

Subversive journalism
Gonzo revolution
Up the establishment
Cabal and pact
Bill's scheme
The ersatz and ubiquitous
Source and CI
Bob Fowler
Juicy quotes
Worked into stories
The Globe and Herald
Mainstream press
From me
A Stones fan from Allston
Nobby
Part of an investigative team
A booster from Brockton
Bill wrote
A locksmith from Lowell
Hilarity shared
Breaking the rules
Talk of the times
By any means necessary
Before misinformation
Became fashionable
Like Fox news
Weapons of mass destruction
Not a hipster gag
Started a war

Harry Bikes

Knock on the door
Murder Building
Cambridge
David Felton
Rolling Stone reporter
Cardoso's roommate
From San Francisco
In town researching
Fort Hill
Mel Lyman gang
Cover story
Knew him when
Filled him in
Straight talk
Ersatz world savior
Banjo playing
Boyfriend of
Kansas City frail
Judy Silver at Brandeis
Broke their hearts
Tragic tale
Later Avatar
Epic struggles
Took Mel's side
Trashed me as
Political thug
Harry Bikes
Hell on earth
No angel
Ran into Felton
Elton John party

In LA
Snake-eyed worm
Weaseling about
Threatened to
Put a hurt on
Egg-sucking
Scumbag

Avatar editors Dave Wilson, left, and Charles Giuliano A.K.A. Harry Bikes.

Chris Burden

Meeting Chris Burden
7/29/89
Private tour
ICA retrospective
Some apprehension
Pulled a knife on TV interviewer
Conceptual piece
Exploring risk and pain
Limits of human endurance
Like "Shoot"
Early work in 1971
Shot in the arm as art
Why I asked
As American as apple pie
Everybody thinks about it
On TV all the time
Country founded on
People shooting people
Why we don't have many
Indian people
Right
560 Americans each week
Facing our worst fear
Done in a clinical way
Injury everyone abhors
But are fascinated by
Just stood there
I like doing something
Quick and powerful
Friend of mine with rifle
Supposed to just graze me

Draw one drop of blood

Pushing it

Can I see the scar

Hesitation

Rolled up his sleeve

Doubting Thomas

As a conceptual art piece Chris Burden had himself shot.
Photo © 2015 Charles Giuliano.

Up the River

Struggling for birth
Merging art and memory
Exploring the horrific
Unknown
Handful of confidantes
Pleased to be among them
Without mercy
Or remorse
I stripe your back
Lash of an overlord
Or editor
Demanding you press on
Further, deeper
Up the river
Into the cave
Where we meet
Then decapitate
Colonel Walter E. Kurtz
The Horror
Drink tea
Swap war stories
Hearts united in darkness
Mine of a domestic nature
By comparison
So benign
Draconian fangs
As you say
Cut just as deep.
Each in our private hell
Assigned there
By Dante

Or Art Forum
From a walk
On the wild side

Spirit Boat. Photo collage © 2015 Charles Giuliano.

All Dolled Up

Beauty parlor today
Semi-annual haircut
Domain of women
No big deal
Used to be a guy thing
Summer buzz cuts
Beaconsfield Hotel
Torn down for condos
Mom gave me a buck
Crossed the trolley tracks
Basement corner
Down the stairs
Man's world
Finished with splash of
Bay Rum
Seventy-five cents
Quarter for tip
The 1970s
Kenny and me
Easter weekend
Defected from Mar 'y' Sol
Rock-fest in Puerto Rico
Flew to Virgin Islands
Small plane down low
Crystal clear Caribbean
Airline, hotel, car
Owned by woman on the mountain
Drinks looking at the bay
Driver to and from the beach
Met Aldo
Hairdresser from Newton

Come see me

First time in a salon

Kindah creepy

Hair washed

Plastic cape with girlie poodles

No one done that before

Lined up with other dames

Slipped him a reefer for a tip

Later at a party

Hey man

No hey man me

After work lit up in his car

Busted

Hey Aldo

Sorry dude

Hostas along the stone wall of our home in Adams. Photo © 2015 Charles Giuliano.

February

Dead of winter
Snow belted
Shoveling out
Slipping and sliding
Slushing about
Bundled up
Wearing me Irish sweater
Netflix nights
Projects by day
Dim light
Sweetie pies
Midst of shortest month
Seed catalogs
Spring comes
Too soon
Most productive
Time of year
Ice melts
Come March

Noah Snowah

Forty days
Forty nights
Not rain but
Snow
Highah and highah
Nowhere to put it
Cities slammed
No school
Makeup days till summah
Wintah
Slippin and slidin
Biblical proportions
Fun if you ski
Shooshboom
Pain in the ass
Otherwise
Come spring
Meltdown
Mud slides
Muckin about
The Gods
Must be angry
Planet
Outah whack
Whammmo

Nobirds

Frost on the pumpkin
Snowbirds
Off and running
Sunbelt
Phoenix to Miami
Mexico or Costa Rica
Barefoot on the beach
Surfin' Safaris
Tans on wrinkled skin
Nobirds
Stay put
Tough it out
Adventurous travel
Home to Big Y
Most days
Going nowhere
Too treacherous
Just doctor and dental
Snow piling up
Setting records
Way it should be
Back in the day
Roots in the cellar
Cabbage and potatoes
Apples in the barrel
No fresh strawberries
Roses for Valentines
World upside down
Messing with nature
Comes with a
Price

East Boston Blizzards

Winters in East Boston
Law of the jungle
Handicapped spots
Handed down for generations
In front of their house
Easy access
Come and go
No problem
Record numbers on Webster Street
Knowing someone who knows someone
Friend of a friend
Joe sent me
Made Man
Gang wars over remaining spots
Shoveled out
Back breaking labor
Claimed with old chairs
Death threats to move them
Even in summer
Stones to protect your turf
Keying offenders
Flattened tires
Tuned up
Fingers crossed
Coming home after dark
Nightmares
Midnight gambling
Or even shopping
Too risky
Hunkered down
Till spring

March

The brawny hands of winter
Choking the breath
Of spring
Persephone returns to frozen earth
Now into March
More frigging snow
Big soft flakes
Falling outside tall loft windows
Dim tones
These first hours of Daylight Saving
Clocks inching forward
Up and down the halls
Neighbors hacking and fevered
Sleep dosed with Nyquil
Tea with lemon and honey
Hydrate she tells me
Week in NY cancelled
Too sick to travel
Mean season
Prolonged beyond reason
Little cheer
Since seasons greetings
Mocking echo
Muffled strangled reverie
Setting records
For utter misery
Must break soon
Melting into epic floods
Curse God
And die

April

Busting out of the cave
Hungry for adventure
Shaking off hibernation
Gathering with critics
In New Orleans
Strolling decadent
Bourbon Street
Where every day
Is Mardi Gras
Visiting haunts of
Tennessee Williams
Corner seat
At restaurant
Across from his place
Drives from loft to home
First growth
Poking up
Spots of color
In brown ground
Then to the Cape
Week on the beach
P' Town getting ready
For summer
Gorging on oysters
Then back to the Berkshires
On the road again
Burning rubber
Highways of the mind

May

Tulip and Magnolia trees
In full bloom
Along Comm Ave
Staying at St. Botolph Club
Spring visit to Boston
Following most brutal
Winter on record
Huge piles of snow
Now gone
Opening night of Pops
Home in the Berkshires
Days warm like summer
Then bitter and mean
How arbitrary
True to New England
Raising then dashing hope
Back road to Pittsfield
First night of summer theater
So lush and green
Rolling hills
Orchard in bloom
Laid out in well-tended rows
Backyard
Working the flower beds
Hands all bashed
Tough getting up and down
Honest peasant labor
Like Sicilian and Irish ancestors
Blunt crude hands
To plant and sow
Still frost at night

When to put in tomatoes
Yet again hopes of harvest
Crops that never flourish
Like Seven Plagues of
Biblical Egypt
Actually
Gorgeous Adams
With stunning view
Across the meadow
Our ever-changing movie
Mt. Greylock

Monty's

Train to Cape Ann
Bus to Annisquam
Alone in the summer house
Spring Break
Working on my boat
Morning drop off at
Addison Gilbert Hospital
Long walk to Monty's
Yard filled
Shed jammed and stacked
Getting a jump
How to get mine down from the loft
Yankee diplomacy
Talk of winter, friends and families
Gradual, when, followed by twinkling, maybe
Today being Monday
Chances of Tuesday, dim
Wednesday, maybe
Thursday, could be
Afternoon say
Gottah clear a path
Ain't easy
Long days alone
Walking cold Lighthouse Beach
Not much in the cupboards
Big can of plums maybe beans
Slim pickins
Visiting Jane Tarr
Fellow skipper in the village
She hosted a sock hop
Fell in love that night

Close dancing to
Stranger in Paradise
Finally, sanding the hull
Downtown for paint and supplies
Gloucester Marine and Lumber
Three coats of hard, slick enamel
Dated a bit that summer
Too busy racing
Boat sure was fast

June

Book launch at the Mount
High energy
Great fun
So many friends
Gathered on the porch
Then a real push
Annual migration
Loft to home
Too many details
Friends asking
When do you move
Finally first night
Morning coffee
On the deck
Breathing nature
In the Berkshires

July

Tight schedule
Worked out
With meticulous detail
Comparing calendars
Juggling openings
Four theatres
Tanglewood
Treasured visits to
Jacob's Pillow
At first exhilarating
Soon routine
Performances merging
Everything a blur
What did you like
People ask
Posting daily
Trying to have a life
Squeezed into rare
Days off
Loving being there
So much to see
When the stars
Come to the Berkshires

www.ingramcontent.com/pod-product-compliance
Lightning Source LLC
Chambersburg PA
CBHW031559110426
42742CB00036B/258

*9 7 8 0 9 9 6 1 7 1 5 1 9 *